"Churches must reengage with their neighborhoods. This book presents a model for a church that overcomes the nightmares of urban traffic and builds community in local spaces. I encourage you to read this book to spark your imagination for what new shapes the church might embody."

—Kurt Fredrickson, DMin, PhD
Associate Dean for Doctor of Ministry and
Continuing Education
Assistant Professor of Pastoral Ministry
Fuller Theological Seminary
Pasadena, CA

"The historic urban church has served to bring hope and joy to centuries of inner-city Christians across our nation. As urban centers continue to populate, parking spaces are almost impossible to find and gridlock causes commuting times to increase, so many would-be worshippers are less inclined to attend church. This, according to Dr. Michael Donaldson, is a major obstacle to many urban dwellers.

His solution is small groups of Christians hosting Sabbath services and weeknight small groups in close proximity to viable transportation hubs. Dr. Donaldson's church is a test platform for community building in overly populated metropolises. What's new with his model? It places small meta or cell groups in strategic areas to maximize the effectiveness and efficiency of marketplace ministries outside the traditional church building. So far this experiment in efficiency is yielding positive results."

—Dr. Alan N. Keiran
Captain, Chaplain Corps, USN (Ret.)
Chief of Staff, US Senate Chaplain's Office
Washington, DC
Author of *Take Charge of Your Destiny* and *Don't Be Surprised*

"I have been privileged to know Mike Donaldson for twenty-five years. We have enjoyed a great working relationship. I have found him to be dedicated and zealous in every undertaking that he has pursued. He served as the International Youth President of the Apostolic World Christian Fellowship. The AWCF is a worldwide ministerial alliance consisting of over twenty-one thousand member ministers in fifty-four nations, representing more than five million laity. Mike Donaldson has brought his scholarship, dedication, and expertise to this literary offering. I suggest that for anyone who is a serious student, pursuing excellence, Mike Donaldson's book is a must read."

—Bishop Samuel L. Smith
General Chairman
Apostolic World Christian Fellowship

"In a day when the mega-church seems to be the order of the day, it is good to be reminded that a building does not constitute the church. The people do. Mike Donaldson shows us that even in this iPhone, iPad, Facebook, LinkedIn, Twittering, e-mailing age of the twenty-first century, we can still learn from and model the first-century church.

As in the Book of Acts, by strategically using small groups and the transport system of the area, Mike is indeed taking the church to the people instead of having the people come to the church. In other words, he has it "all MAPT out."

—Don diXon Williams
African American Church Relations
Bread for the World
Washington, DC

SMALL GROUPS
BIG CITY

EXPRESS LANES TO CHURCH COMMUNITY

SMALL GROUPS
BIG CITY

DR. MICHAEL A. DONALDSON
FOREWARD BY JOEL COMISKEY

TATE PUBLISHING
AND ENTERPRISES, LLC

Published by Tate Publishing & Enterprises, LLC
127 E. Trade Center Terrace | Mustang, Oklahoma 73064 USA
1.888.361.9473 | www.tatepublishing.com

Tate Publishing is committed to excellence in the publishing industry. The company reflects the philosophy established by the founders, based on Psalm 68:11,
"The Lord gave the word and great was the company of those who published it."

Published in the United States of America

ISBN: 978-1-62024-429-6
1. Religion / Christian Church / Administration
2. Religion
12.05.30

DEDICATION

To my parents, Roger and Ruby Donaldson,
who provided the framework for living my
life in an honorable and godly manner

ACKNOWLEDGMENTS

First and foremost, I would like to thank the Lord Jesus Christ for providing the creative idea for this book, the determination to persevere while writing, and the stamina and encouragement to complete the process.

Gratitude is extended to the entire management and staff of Tate Publishing & Enterprises, LLC, for their insight and cooperation in publishing and marketing this book.

To the Washington, DC, metropolitan area and Washington Beltway Community Church, which respectively serve as the pilot city and congregation for testing and implementing the strategic model written about in this book. My prayer is that what has been done here will be an inspiration for other churches in cities around the world.

I would also like to thank the city planners, transportation agencies, and their employees in the

Washington, DC, metropolitan area and throughout the world. All of these dedicated people operate and maintain our transportation systems, roadways, and interstates as they make our lives better as we commute for various purposes, but they receive mostly criticism from the general public and little thanks.

My eternal thanks is bestowed upon my wife, Christy Donaldson, who read, offered constructive editorial comments, and supported me unselfishly throughout the duration of writing this book. I could not have asked for a more supportive ministry and life partner.

Finally, I would like to thank the readers of this book who desire to explore fresh, new methodologies to empower their congregations, denominations, and communities to experience deeper relationships with each other and with God.

TABLE OF CONTENTS

FOREWORD

I met Michael Donaldson in 2003 when he visited me in Moreno Valley, California. At that time, he attended my own Thursday cell group in my house, and afterwards we talked excitedly about church growth through cell ministry on a worldwide scale. I discovered that Michael was already a student of the worldwide cell movement and had done a lot of personal study and onsite research on and in growing cell churches around the world. I realized that Michael was passionate about discovering keys for Spirit-led church growth through growing cell churches.

Michael's passion to find and discover those keys took him to Fuller seminary, where he eventually earned his doctorate degree and wrote his dissertation on reaching the major cities through small group ministry.

I had the privilege of being one of Michael's "dissertation readers" and immediately detected that I was holding in my hands a work that needed to be published. In his dissertation, Michael set forth breakthrough insight about reaching the major cities through multiplying small groups. I was also impressed by the depth of Michael's understanding of the theological base for New Testament small groups, patterned after the primitive house churches.

I'm excited to say that you now have a simplified, edited version of Dr. Donaldson's dissertation in your hands. You'll discover in this book how to establish holistic small groups at key transportation sectors in major cities (starting in the most congested one: Washington, DC) so that busy travelers can experience biblical community in their normal path of travel. So often we ask busy city workers to attend small groups at faraway locations at inconvenient days and hours. Dr. Donaldson has devised what he calls the DOT model to help solve this problem.

Paul the apostle also focused on major city centers by planting house churches among influential home owners who in turn won their *oikos* connections. The early church, in fact, was born in a cell movement that converted homes into churches and then gathered those groups into a common celebration service when feasible. This is exactly what Dr. Donaldson is promoting in this book, but in a different context and culture.

This book not only defines this new strategy but goes back into the biblical base for small groups, and the reasons why we first need to reach the city centers, just like the apostle Paul. Some small group writers, in their quest to be creative, end up watering down the quality of cell ministry, but Dr. Donaldson's DOT model seeks to combine the quality of the cell with the relevance of modern day city life.

My hope is that you will not only glean small group insights from this book but that you will go forth and practice them in your own life and ministry.

—Joel Comiskey, PhD
Founder and Director of Joel Comiskey Group
www.joelcomiskeygroup.com

INTRODUCTION

Planes, Trains, and Automobiles was a comedy film released in November 1987; its plot involved an advertising executive trying to get back home to Chicago after a business trip to New York. A trip that should have taken approximately two hours by taxi and airplane took three days using almost all modes of transportation, as misfortunes repeatedly happened. The plot of the movie may resonate with commuters in major metropolitan cities who experience the challenges of airport delays, overcrowding on public transportation systems, and traffic congestion on the interstates. These inconveniences result in delays, lost revenue, and the inefficient use of a precious commodity: time. Help is needed to navigate through this seemingly paralyzing gridlock.

Traffic reporting has become an industry to assist people on their commutes to and from work or wherever they may be traveling. High Occupancy Vehicle

17

(HOV) lanes exist to encourage carpooling; toll roads and hot lanes are springing up everywhere as motorists are asked to pay for the convenience of traveling more efficiently. Public transportation, in the form of subways and buses, is encouraged to reduce the volume of traffic, with some employers subsidizing the costs. More roads have been built; lanes have been widened; trains, cars, and buses have been added to the fleet. Yet traffic congestion grows exponentially, the transportation infrastructure becomes more crippled, and frustration abounds. In spite of these challenges, we continually search for express lanes to arrive at our destinations quicker. Whether that is taking a non-stop flight, an express bus or train, or can be as simple as call ahead seating at a restaurant or using express check-out lanes in a grocery store.

Small Groups, Big City: Express Lanes to Church Community was written primarily for the audience of the faith community, including pastors, leaders, and church members. However, many of these concepts may be transferable to the business, governmental, and nonprofit sectors. As you read this book, I invite you to use your imagination to translate its concepts to your environment.

Churches in urban population centers are not immune to the ramifications of a crippled transportation infrastructure. This fallout can be witnessed in tardiness or the decline in church attendance (especially midweek services), cultivation of relationships with other believers, member participation, and financial contributions. Pastoral care and evangelistic efforts are minimized; there is underutilization of spiritual gifts for body ministry and lost time and sleep for the individuals. While a healthy, vibrant, evangelistic church is the goal of any congregation, one must now consider the consequences of traffic congestion for the parishioners in their community, especially those situated in major urban centers on the planet. This is true for an established church, a newly formed congregation, or a future church-planting initiative.

The focus of this book is that there is a solution to traffic congestion that churchgoers experience in cities across the globe. This solution can be found both in decentralizing the church into small groups and in the very modes of transportation that cause the problem in the first place.[1] There are two main goals of this book. The first is to inspire readers to pursue strategies that will facilitate community for congregations and their members among the challenges of urbanization and traffic congestion by identifying prime locations for the formation of these groups along the transportation infrastructure. More importantly, the second goal is to inspire you to see that small groups in the marketplace (using the strategy presented in this book) not only facilitates community among Christians but positions you for evangelism to reach those who do not know Jesus Christ.

Community and evangelism are the goals, it is not an "either or" but a "both and" approach. To achieve small group community and not have them evangelistic in nature, results in the failure of the Church's ultimate purpose. However, evangelistic small groups will feed back into the small group structure, strengthen community and fulfill the Great Commission of Jesus Christ to the Church to make disciples. Reaching these two goals will bring a sense of accomplishment knowing that God used you, the small group members and the local church for the kingdom, for such a time as this.

These topics are addressed in this book by presenting a strategy for creating a regional transportation-based network of small groups by exploring a new, small-group model that I have labeled the DOT Small Group (Cell) Model[SM] (DOT Model). The philosophy of the DOT Model can be summarized by the acronym MAPT. MAPT considers the placement of small groups in locations that are *mobile, accessible, proximate,* and *time efficient*; it has three modules: land, air, and water.

To illustrate the applicability of these concepts, I have chosen Washington, DC, where this model has been implemented by Washington Beltway Community Church, as the pilot city. Washington is a representative city of the world to demonstrate the DOT Model as it is home to 5.5 million people.[2] According to the *2011 Urban Mobility Report*, published by the Texas Transportation Institute, Washington has earned the infamous distinction of being the most traffic-congested city in the United States.[3] Washington also has the second busiest rapid transit system in the country in number of passenger trips, after the New York City subway.[4]

However, this strategy has implications beyond Washington, DC, in that this model may be adapted to other cities with churches in similar urban contexts in the United States, such as New York, Los Angeles, Chicago, Dallas-Fort Worth, Philadelphia, Houston, Miami-Fort Lauderdale, Atlanta, or Boston, or smaller cities and rural areas. Internationally, this model may be adaptable to cities such as Tokyo, Seoul, Mexico City, Sao Paulo, Buenos Aires, Lagos, Cape Town, London, Paris, Sydney, Melbourne, or anywhere else in the world. The resources to accomplish this in many global locations already exist. A brief summary of the book will orient the reader as to what follows.

Chapter 1 provides a framework for a particular church to articulate its heritage, purpose, mission, and vision. It is important to identify your church culture before you embark on the journey of implementing a small-group, transportation-based model. This is illustrated by describing the local context of Washington Beltway Community Church. This includes the church's history, reasons and model for forming a church of small groups in Washington, DC, as well as the means for ministry replication. It will then explore the core values of small group ministry of our church, including MAPT, the transportation element for targeting small-group geographic locations.

Chapter 2 discusses the relevance of knowing the larger context of the regional area in which your particular church is situated or that of a future congregation you intend to start. I demonstrate this by closely examining the Washington, DC, metro area and relating those findings to our church's vision. Regional demographics are reviewed, along with the challenges of social networking and urban traffic congestion that can impede small group community. This challenge requires the creation of a new strategy to target small-group geographical locations.

The third chapter centers in on why we need small groups coupled with a transportation model by examining the church's understanding of how relationships are formed by defining key concepts of community, isolation, and church. Community is further explored through the lens of relationships that are shared among and between Divinity, Humanity, and the Church. Transportation theology is articulated as a means to facilitate and experience community in an urban context where isolation, fragmentation, and a flawed transportation network are prevalent.

Chapter 4 discusses the theological and societal justification of small group community and transportation theology. It provides the biblical and historical precedent for small groups that are facilitated by modes of transportation. The underlying theological support is dependent upon the biblical witness of Jethro, Jesus, and the first-century Church. The urban setting of the first-century Church was conducive to marketplace ministry with transportation facilitating community in small groups in homes and in the temple for larger gatherings. These theological justifications from the past provide the bridge to the future and the community of hope in the context for your church, as it did for Washington Beltway Community Church. The information in this chapter may be helpful to you in discussions with your pastor, church boards, denominational leaders, pastoral staff, and church membership at large, especially if you do not currently have small groups in your church, or if you do and they are only within the confines of your church building and not in the marketplace.

In chapter 5 the small-group network strategy of Washington Beltway Community Church is presented for illustrative purposes in an urban context. As there are many small group models that a church may implement, this is only one of many ways it might be designed by a church that does not already have a small group model in place. Each congregation will have to do prayerful research to determine which model works best for their unique congregation. The small group model detailed in this chapter provides an overview of the types, function, and frequency of community groups, curriculum, leadership development, new member assimilation, weekly celebrations, and monthly grand celebrations after launching new celebration centers. What is unique about this small group model is that the relational factor is considered on every level, so that even in a larger church, people have less likelihood of being lost in the crowd but still are connected in the larger scheme of the church, where checks and balances are maintained.

The sixth chapter will detail the design of the transportation-based network strategy by introducing the DOT Model. While the illustration is designed for the Washington, DC, metropolitan area, it can be adapted for your church's ministry situation anywhere in the world, whether that is in an urban or rural area. I provide some helpful hints in chapter 8 on how you can develop this for your area, or if we can be of service to assist you, please contact us. In the Washington, DC, context, I discuss the concept of the DOT Model and the three modules of land, air, and water independently before presenting the integrated version.

Chapter 7 explores the implementation rationale for merging the small group network strategy that you have chosen, discussed in chapter 5 with the delivery system of the transportation-based network strategy that you have adapted, which is presented in chapter 6. Chapter 8 looks at how a pastor, church, or denomination might begin the process of designing a transportation-based small group strategy, such as the DOT Model for their city or region of the world. It also discusses the necessity for a missionary training track as well as evaluating the effectiveness and efficiency of both the small group model and the transportation-based DOT Model to facilitate small group community. Various evaluation methods will be discussed that will yield critical information for assessing what is working, as well as corrective action steps that should be taken. Finally, the book will conclude with a summary of what has been presented and learned for the immediate ministry context, which is applicable to similar urban contexts around the world.

On a personal note, my interest in transportation and studying maps and cities began to develop as an eight-year-old child. Our family traveled frequently on long-distance road trips, long before the days of the Internet, MapQuest, and Global Positioning Devices. I was the navigator, with map in hand, sitting in the front passenger seat with my father driving, while my mother relaxed in the backseat of the car. Not only did I know many of the roads that needed to be traveled by memory, but I searched for new and faster ways to arrive at the destination. From there my fascination went to buses, trains, and airplanes, their schedules, and the venues that host them. As an adult today, it still brings me joy when I am able to explore all the options for domestic and international travel.

My passion and interest in small groups began in 1981, when I was an undergraduate at Marshall University in Huntington, West Virginia. I was browsing in a local Christian bookstore when I stumbled on Dr. David Cho's book *Successful Home Cell Groups*.[5] I purchased the book and read it many times over the years, along with many related books. Cho's book ignited my passion for learning about innovative small groups and pastoral care in the context of ministry, when it was not very popular in the United States.

I have spent the last thirty years researching and studying the small group phenomenon that has exploded throughout Christianity. This research entails not only reading authors on my own but includes research and interviews conducted on the master's and doctoral educational levels, as well as travels to domestic and international destinations to pursue this topic. As a pastor, I have become a practitioner by implementing much of this research into my ministry. My prayer is that the research presented in this book will be a blessing to you, your churches and denominations, and the Church at large scattered throughout the world as you consider the possibilities of small groups in big cities.

PART ONE:
DEFINING YOUR
MINISTRY CONTEXT

CHAPTER 1

DEFINE YOUR CHURCH

You may lead or be a member of established congregations or denominations that are in urban metropolitan cities around the world. These congregations are grappling with the fallout of traffic congestion mentioned in the introduction. Or you may reside in smaller towns and rural areas that can also benefit from the strategies contained within these pages.

Many churches in urban and rural areas may not have small groups in place as part of their ministry strategy. Other assemblies have small groups woven into the church fabric, but they have been confined only to their church building and desire to have more of a relational impact with church members and those in the marketplace who may not be affiliated with a congregation. In either situation, the consideration of a transportation-based network of small groups may be beneficial to you.

Others reading this book have received the call, or are considering starting a church, or churches, for the group that they are affiliated with. Still yet others may be seeking how to adapt such a model for other purposes. While this book is written from a desire to assist the body of Christ, it may have some applicability for other structures. Whatever your purpose for reading this book, I realize that this is an exciting time for you, but please take the time to understand and define your individual church culture and personality before setting sail to adapt the principles mentioned in this book.

As each person is special and made in the image of God, so is each church and the vision that God has for it. We have our own unique DNA, fingerprints, personality, and history, and so does each church. Before you begin the journey of creating a small group-based transportation network for your church, you should know who you are, where you've been, and define where you want to go. In other words, you need to have a clear understanding of the current state of affairs of your church, its history, and its vision for the future.

One of the best ways to accomplish this is to investigate the data available, both internal and external. The internal data relates to your church history, ministry philosophy, and vision and generally can be obtained through written and oral inquiry with other church leaders and members. In terms of the external data it is important to understand the location of your congregation in the general and regional community. What is critical when gathering the external information is that you not only take the snapshot of the current period of time but also obtain future projections for your region. In following this rationale, you are looking at how to be prepared for the expected changes in your region.

God never becomes stagnant in His plan for us as individuals nor His Church that meets in our communities around the planet. He continually desires to expand our horizons, prompting us to develop and grow into our future. In looking forward, we expect God to take us and our churches to the next level, but we also must make preparations to be ready when the time comes.

The question might arise: "I know where to gather the internal information, but what avenues do I explore to obtain the external data for the region in which my church is located?" Some of the information is as close to you as your computer keyboard and can be accessed in minutes and free of charge, except for the investment of a little time. Other sources of data may have to be compiled and purchased at minimal cost through a vendor or a consultant, in which case it could save time. However, in most cases, a hybrid approach is usually recommended.

The answer to the question of where to locate some of the external information may be right under your nose as you read this book. In the illustrative examples in this book, you will discover several possible sources of where to obtain the external information. When reading a book, many people omit reading the endnotes. When reading this book, you will want to look closely at the endnotes, as they contain a wealth of information that might be beneficial for you in the identification of source data that could be relevant for your congregation and region. Of course, depending on what country you live in, you might have similar sources that are labeled differently.

When you have gathered the internal and external data for your assembly and geographic area, you will need to document your findings. This will be helpful for presentations and discussions with others involved in the immediate process or those in a decision-making role. In sharing this data, the intention is to educate others about information not previously realized and for them to corroborate the evidence and most importantly lay the groundwork by creating excitement for why people should buy into the vision. Of course, this is only the first step in the process, but I will discuss the theology, small group design, and transportation strategies later, which should also be incorporated into the overall vision that you will ultimately share.

I place a huge value on the process of documenting the findings in this step and all subsequent steps for the following reasons. First, documentation serves as a benchmark, a blueprint, for transportation-based small group design and a measuring tool to chart your progress as you move through the different phases of the implementation process. Second, it will also serve as your strategy plan if you desire to share this idea with your pastor, church membership, or denominational boards. Third, there is historical value in this documentation if the situation arises that you have to modify your transportation-based small group network. This might be necessary when new transportation infrastructure is introduced into the region or there is a change in your small group design structure. Lastly, if you desire to replicate this model throughout other existing churches in your denomination or future church-planting endeavors, this becomes the prototype that will need to be tweaked, keeping in mind the unique factors of adaption for each city or rural area.

There are many ways to accomplish this task. I will illustrate to those who may be contemplating where to begin by using Washington Beltway Community

Church and its ministry location of Washington, DC. Throughout each phase of the book, this example will provide continuity so that you can see the real-life practicality of the model and how it might be applicable for your church in its geographic environment.

In this chapter, first I provide a brief introduction to the church that provides information about the church's model of operations, theology, and makeup of the leadership team. Second, my goal is to articulate and define foundational key terms of what a small group is about. Third, I provide more detail about the history and origins of the church and reasons for forming, including describing the need for community to combat isolation, fragmentation, and urbanization. Fourth, I detail the theological reasons for forming a church of small groups that includes the ministry need, focus, model, and need for replicating various components of the ministry. Finally, I summarize with a list of core values for small group ministry.

Remember that your history, reasons for being, theology, mission, core values, and God's plan for the future of your church are specific to you and for each church, so be mindful of this as you develop the abstract of your local ministry context. In subsequent chapters of this book, I provide similar illustrations about how the small group model and the DOT Model can possibly be tailored for your area, along with the strategy on how one would merge their small group model with the DOT Model for maximum effectiveness. However, what is important is to lay the foundation first, including being able to articulate it with clarity. Otherwise, you might have mixed results in the implementation phase.

DEFINING WASHINGTON BELTWAY COMMUNITY CHURCH

Washington Beltway Community Church is an urban, multicultural, regional cell church that officially launched in January 2010 in the Washington, DC, metropolitan area after years of preparation. It is designed as a church made up of a network of small groups (cells) with a transportation theme. The church is nondenominational in affiliation, Pentecostal-Charismatic in heritage, and ecumenical in Christian worldview.

A working definition of "cell church" is offered by Dr. Joel Comiskey in his book, *Home Cell Group Explosion: How Your Small Group Can Grow and Multiply*. He writes, "A cell church in everyday terminology is simply a church that has placed evangelistic small groups at the core of its ministry. Cell ministry is not 'another program'; it's the very heart of the church."[6]

Further clarification is needed because the term "small group" can include many types of groups (e.g.,

Bible study), whereas a cell group, although small, has more specificity. In short, all cell groups are small groups, but not all small groups are cell groups. To differentiate the cell from other types of small groups, one must look at purpose. While many small groups, including cell groups, may have a purpose for spiritual edification, discipleship, and pastoral care, one overarching purpose of a cell group that other small groups generally do not have is couched in the "multiplication factor."

Biologically, cells "multiply by dividing" through a process called mitosis. Likewise a cell group in the church seeks to multiply on every level. This means multiplying people in the cell group through evangelistic efforts; allowing them to discover, develop, and use their spiritual gifts; and training and equipping these participants to become leaders and coaches. When a predetermined numerical ceiling of participants has been achieved in the cell, new cells are birthed into existence with new leaders and coaches caring for the cells, and the life cycle is replicated.

Of course other criteria exist. They include, but are not limited to, the senior pastor overseeing the cell ministry by modeling desired behavior in leading a cell, equipping cell leaders, and coaching those leaders. In a traditional church, which has small groups, this responsibility might be delegated to a small group's pastor. Usually when this is the case, there is competition among the various groups for the senior pastor's time and the needed support on a spiritual and financial level.

For the purposes of this book, I define the cell or small group as a weekly gathering of three to ten people that meet in locations other than the church building for the purpose of fostering community, spiritual edification, pastoral care, discipleship, and equipping with the goal of multiplying the group, its group leaders, and coaches at a future time to be determined. Each cell group member is expected to balance the small group wing experience of the church by participating in the corporate wing of worship on Sundays. This corporate gathering, also known as Celebration, happens when multiplication has transpired and constitutes two or more small groups.

As with any church initiative, including this one and yours, it is not for the faint of heart, nor is it an exact science. It must be born out of a love for the harvest and a calling that is orchestrated by the Spirit of God. Our church is led by a husband-and-wife team, with me serving as the senior pastor of the church, while my wife, Christy, functions in many capacities. Both of us have been Christians for decades, have theological education, are ordained with practical experience in ministry, and have secular professional skills, working in the marketplace as managers in the accounting profession.

I will now explore the local ministry setting of our church. This includes the history, reasons, and model for forming a church of small groups in an urban environment, as well as the means for ministry replication. The core values of the church will be detailed, including MAPT, which is the transportation element for targeting small-group geographic locations.

HISTORY: IN THE BEGINNING

The sense of calling to start a multicultural, cell-based, regional church in the Washington, DC, metro area came in June 2004, while I was living in Greensboro, North Carolina. Over the next five and a half years, preparations were made toward the launching of the first church functions, which occurred in January 2010. My preparation included moving to Washington, continued education, legal matters, and most importantly assembling a leadership team.

The initial leadership team was comprised of a multicultural mix of five individuals: four men and one woman. I teamed up with Don Williams, Russ Barbour, Bruce Branch, and my wife, Christy. All five of us are seasoned ministers and have various areas of expertise.

The governance of the church is pastor-led, with the five-member board of directors overseeing the well-being of the church. I serve as the senior pastor, with Don Williams, Russ Barbour, Bruce Branch, and Christy serving as board members. My wife is a CPA and is presently serving as secretary/treasurer of the church.

I assembled this team based on much prayer and the twenty-five-year history of trust in working with Williams, Barbour, and Branch in other ministerial endeavors. Don Williams brings to the board the consciousness of social justice and Christian ecumenicism. He is the director of church relations for an international world hunger relief organization based in Washington, DC, and a board member of a national multidenominational Christian fellowship. Russ Barbour's area of expertise is journalism and communications, and he is a television producer in both Christian and public television. Bruce Branch has military, music, and campus ministry experience. My wife and I, in addition to being theologically trained ministers, are accountants and bring business savvy to assist the church in its operations.

The leadership team is representative of the diversity of the membership that it hopes to reach. The pastor and his wife are an interracial couple representing African American, Caucasian, and Latin heritage. Don Williams and Bruce Branch are African Americans; and Russ Barbour is Caucasian. These five individuals have many years of experience working in and with multicultural groups.

ISOLATION, FRAGMENTATION, AND URBANIZATION: IT IS NOT GOOD TO BE ALONE

It was God who said in Genesis 2:18, "It is not good that man should be alone."[7] To rectify this situation, He gave Adam a wife and later children. As humanity increased numerically over centuries, we now have the possibilities of relationships with family, friends, and colleagues. In short, God never wants anyone to live in isolation but to have interconnectivity and interrelatedness with others, experiencing life together.

Unfortunately, sociologically as a whole, the "country culture" of the United States is individualistic in nature, as opposed to some other cultures around the world who live life together interdependently with the family or larger community at the center. George Gallup Jr. concluded from his studies and polls that Americans are among the loneliest people in the world.[8] This is of particular interest because we find ourselves conducting ministry in the capital of the United States.

This is not to say that we in the United States do not value our immediate family or friends, but corporately as a nation, our vision is narrowly centered.

Following an individualistic philosophy, in most cases, will net the results of the needs of the one or the few outweighing the needs of the many. This approach not only lends itself to isolation but fragmentation as well.

Fragmentation is a sense of "being apart" from the whole. This separateness can be traced by many identifying factors on a national scale including, but not limited to, race, ethnicity, religion, denomination, education, class or social status, sex, political party affiliation, and income. On the local level, many do not even know their next-door neighbors, regardless of what they might have in common.

When the focus of our lens is narrowed, the family system is fragmented. The family is the cornerstone of civilization. The divorce rate in the United States is approximately 50 percent.[9] Every year, approximately one million children become part of a single-parent home, and the percentage of children under eighteen living with a single parent is 28 percent.[10] Those that are in this place should never be shunned but cared for, loved, and engrafted into extended families. However, fragmentation is not limited to families that have split up; it exists in so-called "traditional families."

In traditional or model families, there is a battle inwardly that is warred with fragmentation. Various factors can contribute to this state of affairs, such as two-wage earner households, schedule conflicts, dietary requirements, and ownership of separate vehicles and entertainment devices. It can be a rare occurrence when a family is able to have a regular meal together most days of the week.

Fragmentation, therefore, is prevalent everywhere in our society, regardless of what our family or other descriptive classifications might be. While it is likely to be less of a problem in rural communities, the fact remains it still exists. In cities such as yours and mine in Washington, DC, it is probably intensified because of urbanization.

Simply stated, urbanization is the process of cities originating and growing. This ministry is located in such an area with approximately five and a half million people. Census information for the Washington metropolitan region illustrates recent urban growth in this community, with populations of 3,478,000 in 1980; 4,223,000 in 1990; and 4,923,153 in 2000.[11] The actual results from the recent 2010 US Census indicate that an estimated number of 5,582,170 people live in the metro region.[12] The population increase from 1980 to 2010 is 2,104,170 people, representing growth of 60 percent during this thirty-year period.

The speed and degree of urbanization in most cities around the world, as in the Washington, DC, metro area, can be attributed to factors noted in the research performed by Roger S. Greenway and Timothy M. Monsma, authors of *Cities: Missions' New Frontier.*

They list eight dynamics of urbanization, namely: government, education, health care, information, entertainment, trade, industry, and warfare.[13] While most cities have a majority of these dynamics, few have all of them. Washington, DC, as the seat of the federal government and home to foreign embassies from countries around the world, can lay claim to them all.

Urbanization can provide opportunities to connect to countless numbers of people and develop meaningful relationships. It may also have an impact that impairs the trust needed to develop friendships, and it desensitizes the concern for others. Many who relocate from smaller towns to a cosmopolitan city such as Washington or where you live may find it difficult to adjust and find themselves all alone in the midst of millions of people.[14] Some who have lived in urban cities their entire lives experience the same feelings of loneliness for various reasons. It is not good for anyone to be alone, and one way to combat isolation and fragmentation in your region is by using small groups that nurture community. That is what we have done here in Washington, DC.

FORMING A CHURCH OF SMALL GROUPS: ON THIS ROCK, I WILL BUILD MY CHURCH

Jesus declared, "On this Rock I will build my Church and the gates of Hades will not prevail against it" (Matt.

16:18). The prophetic fulfillment of the Church came on the Day of Pentecost, which was shortly after His death, resurrection, and ascension. The Church has been in existence, now, for almost two thousand years.

Your assembly, and ours here in Washington, cannot and does not seek to rebuild the Church; rather, it is only the continuation of the Church in this part of the vineyard in this age. The leadership team of our church see our role as facilitators to combat isolation and fragmentation in this urban ministry setting, thereby being a conduit where people can be in relationship with one another and, more importantly, where people and God can be in mutual relationship. Our contention is that this can be best accomplished by meeting in small groups. More will be discussed later in this book about the theology and mechanics of the small groups. The remaining portion of this section will elaborate on the ministry need for our church in Washington, DC, along with the ministry focus, ministry model, and ministry replication aspects. For you that have not considered this yet, the objective is to assist you and your church in defining your ministry need, focus, model, and replication philosophy.

MINISTRY NEED

The Washington metropolitan region is quite extensive in area and includes the District of Columbia and parts of the states of Maryland, Virginia, and West

Virginia. As of 2010, the population of the area is estimated at 5,582,170.[15] The population is expected to increase through 2016.[16] In chapter 2, detailed demographic information will be presented for the wider context of the Washington region; however, for now the expected continued growth of the National Capital Region constitutes just one reason for the need for additional churches to be started in this area. The goal of this church, and any other, should be to reap the expected harvest, ushering souls into God's kingdom.

The Washington metropolitan area is part of a larger region called, for statistical purposes, the Baltimore-Washington metropolitan area and, as of the 2010 US Census, this area had an estimated population of 8,924,087.[17] The Baltimore-Washington metropolitan area statistics are included in this ministry need analysis for the following three reasons. First, Baltimore is approximately thirty-three miles from Washington, DC, and there is a transient component that lives in the Baltimore metropolitan region yet commutes for employment opportunities in the higher-paying Washington, DC, metro area. It is expected that some of these commuters will attend our cell groups during the work week. Second, religious statistics presented in this book are based on the Baltimore-Washington metropolitan region. Finally, the Baltimore region will be considered for a future church plant. As you begin to define the need and vision for your church, think larger than your immediate situation, as we serve a big God who can do exceeding above all that we ask or think.

Another need for this church, beyond overall population growth, is the staggering statistics of the unchurched. Data compiled by the Association of Religion Data Archives (ARDA)[18] reports on the religious congregations and membership affiliations in the Washington-Baltimore metropolitan region as of the year 2000. If you live in the USA you can get this information for your city or region as well. At the time of this writing, the ARDA report does not reflect the results of the 2010 US Census, and I was informed that it would not be available until late 2012, which is beyond the scope of the production of this book. These statistics represent 104 denominations of a total of 188 groups.[19] These 104 denominations are grouped into six theological categories and are comprised of 4,806 congregations and 4,705,050 people in this region. This study represents 61.8 percent of the total region population of 7,608,070 as of the year 2000, of which 4,166,396 people are categorized as not having any church affiliation.[20]

Particular attention can be paid to the unclaimed category—4,166,396 people who have no church affiliation. This number represents 54.8 percent of the total

Washington-Baltimore region. Upon further analysis, historically, African American denominations were not counted. However, when these are considered and extrapolated, there are still 2,903,020 people in the unclaimed category, which would translate into 38.2 percent of the population without church affiliation.

With the latest data provided as of the 2010 Census, it is estimated that the Baltimore-Washington metro area has a population of 8,924,087.[21] For illustrative purposes, using the assumption that the 38.2 percent ratio for the unclaimed category in the 2000 ARDA survey remains unchanged, that would mean that 3,409,001 people have no church affiliation as of 2010. Projecting to the year 2016, this number could climb higher than 3,463,545, using the anticipated growth factor. It is because of this three million-plus people in the unclaimed or unchurched category that the need for starting a church arises. I am convinced that this church can tap into a small segment of this population with the message of hope. Your church can do the same as well, but as you define your church, you must not look at the present only; you must project and accommodate for future growth of the geographic region in every way.

The final reason for beginning the church is the establishment and nurturing of healthy relationships. These relationships focus on our relationship with

God, each other as Christians, unbelievers, and the community at large. I suggest the best way to accomplish this task is through vibrant small groups rather than the church-building-centric model. It is also through this vehicle that pastoral care, evangelism, and accountability can flourish.

The need for starting the church validates the very mission to fulfill that need. Our mission, and we do choose to accept it, is to "go into all the world and preach the Gospel to every creature" (Mark 16:15, KJV). The same God that said, "Come unto me," said, "Go unto them." Our mission statement refines the Great Commission into practical application. It reads:

> The mission of Washington Beltway Community Church is to serve God by serving you through the vehicle of small groups. Our goals are to:
> - Promote an intimate, personal relationship with the Lord Jesus Christ and other members of the body of Christ
> - Encourage spiritual growth and leadership opportunities for men and women
> - Provide personalized pastoral care
> - Reach our community through lifestyle evangelism[22]

The vision for Washington Beltway Community Church is to have a multicultural, cell-based, regional church in the Greater Washington, DC, metropolitan area that comprises a sixty-mile radius. This defined target area includes the City of Washington, DC (proper), and the suburban areas located in Maryland and Virginia. Our outlook is articulated by our vision statement, which reads: "Washington Beltway Community Church is a multicultural, Spirit-filled church of small groups through which we promote relationships, spiritual growth, pastoral care, and evangelism."[23]

If you do not have a mission and vision statement for your church, I would recommend that you brainstorm with the leadership of your church to develop them. A lot of prayerful consideration should go into the process. This will describe to your congregation, prospective converts, and the community at large what you see as your church's task in the world and how you are going to accomplish this task.

MINISTRY FOCUS

The ministry focus group is the target market that your church will be seeking to reach with evangelistic efforts. Focus groups and target markets have their roots deeply embedded in the business discipline of marketing. For our church in Washington, briefly stated, our target market is everyone, and our focus is having a multicultural congregation. However, we will be looking to start with those who live, work, or attend universities within the Capital Beltway proximity and expand to a sixty-mile radius of Washington, DC.

The widespread school of thought and literature of starting churches has suggested generally that ministry focus groups be based upon a philosophy of homogeneity or likeness.[24] This philosophy seeks to reach those whom the planters or existing congregations have "likeness with" in ethnicity, education, age, social status, cultural values, financial position, and political affiliation, among other criteria that may exist. Sociologists have statistically identified classes of people that are to be most likely affiliated with a particular denomination by keying in on these demographic traits.

While there has been some evidence to suggest that homogeneous target markets for ministry can be successful, Hozell C. Francis addresses some concerns about the homogeneous unit principle in his book *Church Planting in the African-American Context.* It may be beneficial for readers to understand his concerns in order to see why we as Christians need to move to reach a heterogeneous or diverse types of people in our churches. He writes:

> First, if new believers begin with their "own kind," will they not be inclined to remain with them and thereby perpetuate a segregated Christianity?

Second, will not many see the homogeneous principle as an excuse for not reaching people, simply because of difference in race, religion, language, or the like? Many believers have regular contact with people who may have one or more distinctives. Yet they communicate about matters such as politics, sports, or family concerns. Why not do the same in matters of religion?

Third, homogeneity may give credence to those who hold a notion of superiority with respect to race, education, language, or other cultural identifiers. It may offer support to the segregationist efforts in a number of these categories, especially at the popular level of racial superiority.

Finally, as neighborhoods and communities change, churches that do not assimilate their community in an all-inclusive manner will suffer extinction.[25]

The homogeneous unit principle was not the biblical model that Jesus or the apostles employed for the evangelization of their world. It is clear that neither this church, nor any other church, can reach all the unchurched in the Washington, DC, metro area. The important question is, "What would Jesus or the apostles have done under similar circumstances?" I suggest that they would and did promote a church that was multicultural, and whoever received the Gospel was welcome regardless of ethnicity, age, education, and social status. Jesus recruited a varied group of individuals, including professionals (a doctor and a tax collector) as well as trade laborers, carpenters, and fishermen.

The Church started on the Day of Pentecost with sixteen nations gathered together in Jerusalem to witness the event (Acts 2:8-11). It was a multicultural, multilingual experience. The Gospel message then spread to Samaria (Acts 8:14-16), whose constituents were biracial. Next it went to the entire region of Judea, including the Gentile household of Cornelius (Acts 10:1-48), and finally then the Apostle Paul took the Gospel to the world of his day (Acts 13-28).

Jesus's birth, death, and resurrection were for all humanity. Jerry Appleby and Glen Van Dyne, authors of the book *The Church Is in a Stew: Developing Multicongregational Churches*, quote Ray Bakke, a recognized authority on multicultural ministry in urban settings, about the contribution of Jesus Christ. They write, "The Good News is not only that Jesus shed his blood for the world, but also that he got his blood from the world. That is good news especially in a racist society, in a world of yellow, black and brown people."[26] Jesus did not come to redeem one class of people but made salvation available for all. When on earth, He reached out not only to Jews but to Samaritans, women, the poor, the affluent, the educated, as well as the illiterate. When Jesus died,

He broke down not only the middle wall of partition (Eph. 2:14) that separated the Jew and Gentile but any other measure of division that could ever be conceived in the heart of humanity. While it is true that Jesus and the apostles experienced numerous challenges in targeting a multicultural market, they did not shrink from their mission to target a specific group of people. They accepted the challenge, and so does Washington Beltway Community Church.

All true ministry results from a compassion for people and a desire to show our love, as well as God's love, to them. This is the case, whether there is a specific target market or one that is broad in scope, as in a multicultural context. However, the church that targets a multicultural, all-inclusive target market seeks to send a message, not only to the Church, but to the rest of the world (especially the unchurched) that the love of God is truly real and is being demonstrated. It is a powerful witness when the world (Church and unchurched alike) can see people coming together from various ethnic groups, professions, educational levels, political affiliations, and socioeconomic statuses on a regular basis, worshipping God and being in communion with each other. It will be an attractive feature of a "hermeneutic (interpretation) of love," more powerful than any sermon that could ever be preached. Jesus summed it up best when He said, "By this shall all men know that you are my disciples, if you have love for one another" (John 13:35).

MINISTRY MODEL

The general ministry model that our church embraces is the cell-celebration model, and is what I write about in this book. Although I highly recommend this model, you will have to determine what works best for your congregation. Within this cell church model are various sub-models that have been adapted to facilitate the functionality of the cells or small groups.[27] The sub-model that our congregation has implemented is the DOT Small Group (Cell) Model. The nucleus of the vision of the cell-celebration model resides in the concept of small groups (cells), which meet weekly outside of a church building at different locations and on various days and times. These microcosmic cells are the focal point, life, and bloodline of Washington Beltway Community Church, rather than the more traditional Sunday morning corporate gathering of believers, which we call "Cell-e-bration." This is a play on the word *celebration* (which most cell churches name their Sunday morning service) to provide a naming identifier to the cell church model. The celebration service on Sundays will bring together all of the cell groups scattered throughout the metropolitan area for corporate worship and fellowship on a larger scale, with the understanding that real life and Christian community exists on the small group level.

Washington Beltway Community Church is not a church *with* small groups but a church *of* small groups, because the small groups are the essence of the Church. The life lived out in the cells spills over into the celebration. In the cell church structure, the focus changes from crowd-to-core (dominant style in the traditional church model) to core-to-crowd.

It is in these small groups where relationships will be nurtured, new believers assimilated, pastoral care administered, gifts exercised, as well as equipping and training conducted. They will serve as a vehicle for evangelism to reach and assimilate non-Christians. The cell group is also a vehicle that "closes the back door," so that new Christians may be more easily retained. More will be said in chapter 5 about the size, function, and frequency of the cells when the small group network strategy is discussed. Our ministry flowchart is depicted in figure 1.1 below.

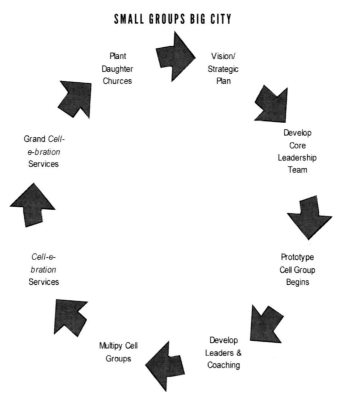

Figure 1.1 - Washington Beltway Community
Church Ministry Flowchart

MINISTRY REPLICATION

In chapter 1 of Genesis, it was God who said, "Be fruitful and multiply." Robert Logan explains this principle in writing, "From the beginning, God intended for us to multiply. Everything that is living and healthy is designed to multiply: animals, plants, people."[28] God also desires that our ministries not only be fruitful but multiply, and this should be our desire as well. This would include small groups, cell leaders, coaches, pastors, and churches. The goal of Washington Beltway

Community Church is not to become a mega-church with multiple small groups with one primary leader but to become many smaller congregations with multiple cell leaders, coaches, and pastors who continue to replicate themselves, providing continuity and opportunities for pastoral care, evangelism, and equipping. Again, each church has its own structure and DNA, so what is applicable for our church may not be what you envision for yours.

Our strategy for multiplication includes suggesting that new converts immediately participate in small groups, enroll in the leadership training track, eventually become an apprentice of a small group, and finally lead their own small group with the full support of the church. Small Groups, which we call community groups, are a predetermined size, and multiplication of these small groups will be deliberate with a target date of birthing a new small group. Mentoring and formal coaching of new small-group leaders will be the responsibility of the leader of the cell from which the birthing of the new small group took place.

Celebration services should be birthed after a predetermined number of community groups are formed. Celebrations will have a predetermined size before new congregations are started with a new pastor. Grand Celebrations are the coming together of multiple congregations for fellowship and edification.

More will be said in chapter 5 about the multiplication strategy, types of groups, and numerical values of multiplication of the various facets of the ministry. The multiplication of cells, leaders, coaches, and pastors will be carried out utilizing the DOT Model discussed in chapter 6.

While many churches seek to maintain the status quo by quarantining their members and leaders, the leadership of our church desires to empower members by offering both education and on-the-job training, coaching, and sending them out to participate in ministry. We want to serve as a resource of encouragement to the network of small groups and churches. This is true regardless of whether, at a later date, some of the members or daughter churches decided to fellowship elsewhere.

It would be wonderful if a church could retain all its converts, but this is usually not the case, as many move on either to other locations around the world or to other churches in the region where your church is based. In our area, Washington is a cosmopolitan, transient city, political capital of the United States, home of at least nineteen universities, multiple military bases of each of the branches of the armed forces, and 173 foreign embassies. This region is ripe to promote world evangelism without one ever leaving the city. For this reason, we will have a missionary training aspect that incorporates the foundations of the

DOT Model for church members that relocate to other cities or countries and desire to start a church. As you prayerfully consider the option of a transportation-based small group system for your church, please do not overlook the extended possibilities that might exist in other areas in your immediate region or develop internationally.

While we expect some to leave our assembly and go to other churches in the Washington area, it is our conviction that by promoting a "freedom-of-choice" philosophy that God gives to each of us, many will willingly desire to maintain fellowship with our congregation. For those that desire to leave the formal network, our wish is to maintain fellowship as a family of believers. Many churches have alienated former members and leaders in retaliation for their decision to move on, but we view it as part of the maturation process, as when a child becomes an adult, makes decisions about his or her life, but still can have a relationship with the family of origin in which mutual respect and love prevail.

CORE VALUES OF SMALL GROUP MINISTRY: INCARNATIONAL MINISTRY AT YOUR SERVICE

Jesus was God incarnate and came to minister by giving of Himself and serving others. This is what is desired for the church: a life of service. The motto of Washington Beltway Community Church is: "Serving

Christ by Serving You." We have established seven core values for our church, as presented in table 1.1.

These core values of our church reflect its small group philosophy and commitment to ministry. Community is relational; pastoral care is concern for others; evangelism is sharing our faith; empowerment for service is equipping believers; multiplication is the mathematical mandate to be fruitful and reproduce; inclusiveness accepts everyone; and MAPT is respect for our members. If you have not as yet, you probably should draft and document the core values of your church, as it tells people what is important to your congregation and how they might identify with your church.

Core Value	Description
Community	Emphasis on developing and nurturing relationships with each other and with members of society at large
Pastoral Care	Prioritization of ministry to pastoral needs (sickness, death, encouragement, counseling, etc.)
Evangelism	Focus outwardly on the needs of non-Christians, rather than having an inward maintenance mentality
Empowerment for Service	Assist all persons in developing their God-giftings (equipping and training) providing a forum for the utilization of those gifts
Multiplication	Expect and assist all small groups (cells), cell leaders, prayer intercessors, coaches, and every function of the church to be reproductive and reproduce after its own kind
Inclusiveness	Value inclusion and be proponents of multiculturalism and supporting equal opportunities for men and women to participate in leadership regardless of age, sex, ethnicity, culture, socio-economic, and educational status
Mobility, Accessibility, Proximity, and Time Considerations (MAPT)	Meet together at locations that respect accessibility, mobility, proximity (to home, work and school) and time consideration factors of each person in this congested urban context

Table 1.1 – Core Values of Washington Beltway Community Church

CONCLUSION

This chapter introduced the importance for each assembly, regardless of its stage of development or methodology of ministry, to define and document their understanding of the history, status quo, and vision of the future for their church. Each church should consider its uniqueness and God's plan for them before moving to take the steps of working toward creating a transportation-based network of small groups. For the benefit of those who have not had the opportunity to write such a document, I provided you with a possible template to use by sharing the one for our church in the Washington, DC, metropolitan area.

Chapter 2 will explore the challenges to community in the larger context of the region in which a particular church is situated. This is accomplished by analyzing the region through demographic data and other tools available. Factors that impede small group community will be explored, including traffic congestion.

CHAPTER 2

DEFINE YOUR REGION AND CHALLENGES TO COMMUNITY

In chapter 1, I encouraged you to provide an introduction to your assembly on a micro level. This included documenting the history, ministry philosophy, and vision for your church prior to engaging in the process of developing a transportation-based network of small groups. Again, this is important in order for you to have foundational clarity about where you have been and where you intend to go.

This chapter takes a look at the portrait on a macro level, where your local church is engaged in ministry. Not only are the immediate church's culture and practices important, but how will that church's culture and ministry approach fit into the regional area in which it ministers? Questions to be answered for your area might include demographic information on how many people are within your reach? What age and economic bracket are they in? Do they drive or take public transportation? What type of families do they have?

As far as the dynamics of the area itself, questions should be asked and answered to administer your church's vision. They possibly could include: What type of region is it: metropolitan, small city, or rural? What are the main economic factors that shape the area? Is it a center of tourism, manufacturing, agricultural, or financial activities? Does the area thrive on political, cultural, military, or entertainment dynamics? Is it a college town where education is known as its claim to fame? Could it possibly be a region that has embraced clinical medicine, research, or technology?

Whatever the answers to these and other questions are, you should ask them so that your church can understand the unique identifiers in order to address the needs of the people. This also is a requirement before creating a transportation-based small group model for your church. Underlying all of these individual and church identifiers is the goal to create authentic community for you, your congregations, and denominations with the purpose of reaching out to individuals not yet in the community of believers.

To create real community, a church should not only look at the aspects which solidify the larger regional setting but also what the challenges are to create relational community within the larger context. A few of them may be diversity, isolation, and traffic congestion, which this book addresses. Can you think of other challenges to community where you live?

What follows in this chapter is an illustration of how you begin to explore the similarities and challenges in the regional area where your church is, or will be, located. I demonstrate this by identifying the dynamics of the Washington, DC, metropolitan area, through the lens of the history and vision for the area that was embraced by Washington Beltway Community Church. One of our core values stated in the last chapter, and most likely one of yours, is the desire to achieve and see authentic community. In this chapter, the challenges to community in our region are explored, including demographics, social networking, traffic congestion, and the necessity for creating a new approach for performing ministry.

DEMOGRAPHICS

To effectively reach a target market with a message or product, the dynamics of the marketplace should be studied in order to make the appropriate pitch. Corporations invest millions of dollars in demographic studies and surveys to tailor their product to the consumer. The Church has the greatest product and message of all and should be proactive, as well, to reach those with the greatest need by looking at demographic data.

I would like to reemphasize what was discussed in chapter 1: our church is multicultural and not based on the homogeneous unit principle (trying to reach a similar type of person). Our target market is everyone, but knowing the specifics of one's market can only enhance the approach and delivery of the message. The Apostle Paul summarized this approach as he became a Jew, Gentile, and all things to all people, that by all means he might save some (1 Cor. 9:20-22).

Chapter 1 provided a high level of demographic data for the region, including population, expected overall growth, and numbers of those who are connected to a particular religious denomination or unaffiliated with any church. Chapter 2 will explore the demographics of the ministry area at a more granular level including: population and growth by sex, race, and age; households and growth by age, familial structure, and income; housing status and valuations, educational attainment, daytime demographics (employers, businesses, and payroll); and employment, drive time, and mode of transportation, which will be a major factor in proposing the DOT Model. The source data used to understand these demographics originate from actual statistical information from the 2010 US Census, compiled by the US Census Bureau.

I desired not only for our church to look at 2010 demographic information, but to have statistically accurate projections for the next five years (2011-2016) for future planning. As you define your larger region in which you minister, you should do the same. I have the 2011-2016 projections for all the demographic categories listed in this chapter, but for proprietary reasons can only publish in this book data from the 2010 U.S. Census. However, my company, Donaldson and Associates, LLC can provide the current year and five-year projections in various formats for your church, denomination, business, non-profit or government agency for your future planning purposes. Our contact information is in the back of this book.

Geographically, the Washington, DC, metropolitan region is a multistate-jurisdictional area. It includes the District of Columbia and sixteen counties, six of which are in Maryland, nine in Virginia, and one in West Virginia. In Maryland, these counties are Calvert, Charles, Frederick, Montgomery, Prince George's, and Washington. Virginia is represented in the metro region by the counties of Arlington, Clarke, Fairfax, Fauquier, Loudoun, Prince William, Spotsylvania, Stafford, and Warren. West Virginia completes the geographical demographics, with Jefferson County being its lone representative.

I desired a second source of demographic data, which was more descriptive of targeting in on certain geographic areas that would be used in phasing our plan. This profile segregates the original 2010 US Census data and 2011-2016 projections by four radii-strata (ten, twenty, forty, and sixty miles) from the epicenter of the United States Capitol (E. Capitol St. E. and 1st St. NE, Washington, DC 20001). I also made an independent analysis of the four radii-strata that provided the incremental change for each demographic category within each stratum for 2010-2016. This additional information provides our leadership guidance as we target communities and implement the DOT Small Group Model in stages, which will be discussed further in chapter 7.

Using the results of the U.S. 2010 Census information, I am presenting a summary of the major demographic information about the Washington, DC, metro area. Having the five-year projections are important as well, but this should illustrate the usefulness of this data for your church or denomination. To explore every dynamic in detail would make this book voluminous, so only the key demographics are considered in the remainder of this chapter.

POPULATION AND GROWTH
BY SEX, RACE, AND AGE

The total population as of 2010, in the defined statistical area, is 5,582,170[29] and is expected to increase through 2016. The breakdown of the population by sex in 2010 is represented by 2,716,483 males (48.7 percent) and 2,865,687 females (51.3 percent). It is projected that women will still be a majority in the overall population through 2016.[30]

As a cosmopolitan city, Washington is diverse in its ethnicity. In 2010, the population was 54.8 percent white, 25.8 percent black, 0.4 percent Native American, 9.4 percent Asian, 0.1 percent Pacific Islander, 6.0 percent some other race, and those classified as two or more races having 3.7 percent representation. What is interesting is that the statistics now categorize those with two or more races, which debuted in the 2010 Census.[31]

The demographic of age in the metro area is very revealing and in some cases may not be widely known. In 2010, the median age is thirty-six years old. Those thirty-five years old and above represent 52 percent of the population, with the largest age grouping being those between forty-five and forty-nine years old, representing 8.0 percent of the population.[32] What I can say about the period for 2011-2016, is that the church, while being sensitive to all, should be multicultural in approach and not putting those forty and above out to pasture as the region will steadily experience growth in these two areas. Is your church prepared for the future?

HOUSEHOLDS AND GROWTH BY AGE, FAMILIAL STRUCTURE, AND INCOME

In 2010, there were 2,074,730 households in the DC Metro Region, with an average household size of 2.64 people.[33] The definition of a household has sociologically evolved, with the familial structure being ever so diverse. The most prominent size of households in 2010 is a two-person household. Evidence indicates that it does not represent the traditional family that has both parents present and one or more children. This could represent a married couple, cohabiting couples, single or widowed parent with a child parent, two roommates, or any other combination.

The household income in the Washington, DC, area is as diverse as in any other metropolitan city. In 2010 the largest portion (19.9 percent of the population) has annual household income in the range of $100,000 to $149,999 per year. In 2010, the average household income and per capita income is approximately $84,523 and $40,528, respectively.[34]

The church can utilize this data, as it speaks to the reality of hearth and home. The stereotyping of family as nuclear or traditional can no longer be expected. We will have to explore beneath the surface to ascertain how best to minister to different family types while keeping in mind that most householders are forty and over. Income-related data can also provide a glimpse for budget development for the church.

HOUSING STATUS AND VALUATIONS

The residents of the Washington metro area live in a region where real estate prices are generally high. This is true whether one owns or rents property. In 2010, there are a total of 2,213,752 housing units in the region, of which 1,333,662 (60.2 percent) are owner occupied; 741,068 (33.5 percent) are renter occupied units; and 139,022 (6.3 percent) are vacant housing units.[35]

The recent economic recession has not had as severe an impact on the DC Metro Area as other regions, which have more foreclosed properties, so the vacancy rate may be more indicative of the transient nature of the population with the large military and federal government presence. Many of these dwellings are single-family homes, condominiums, duplexes, townhouses, and apartments located in both DC and the suburbs of Maryland and Virginia, but there are generally more apartments and condominiums closer to the District than farther out in suburbia. In many cases, properties in suburbia are located in subdivisions with homeowner or tenant associations. Based on my observations, properties that have more land and are less expensive per square foot the farther they are from downtown Washington. Conversely, as one lives in or closer to the District, the more expensive the property is per square foot. While this seems to be the norm, there are always exceptions.

According to the demographic profile, 1,311,774 homes existed in the Washington metro region. The median home was built in the 1980's, with a median value of $376,200. There were at total of 708,077 rental units and average rent was $1,351.00.[36]

This information is valuable to the church in locating where and how people live, in order to reach them effectively. For ministry that occurs closer to the District, the small group must be tailored to fit the urban lifestyle. This might mean holding small groups in closer quarters or utilizing common areas of condominiums and apartment complexes and using public transportation rather than driving.

EDUCATIONAL ATTAINMENT

Washington is one of the largest population centers in the United States, which attests to having a large number of people that have a post high-school education. In 2010, 69.9 percent of the 3,757,454 above-twenty-five-year-old population had some college or followed through to the completion of their doctoral degree. Those that completed only high school tallied 19.7 percent, while 5.5 percent started but never finished high school. The remaining 4.9 percent has an elementary school education or no education.[37]

Interpreting this data is critical to the strategy that our assembly utilizes in evangelism, discipleship, and equipping. We must bear in mind that we live in an area with a high percentage of people having college education. At the same time, though, we must not alienate those that do not. It may be possible for our church to be instrumental in encouraging those who started high school or some other degree program to complete it.

DAYTIME DEMOGRAPHICS

I recognize, as you do, that the economic lifeblood of any community is the companies that provide jobs at which families can earn a living. In regions where companies are ceasing operations and laying off their workforce, people are sometimes forced to relocate to where the jobs are more plentiful to survive. This has either a positive or negative trickle-down effect to the church economically as well as for member acquisition or retention, depending on the circumstances.

The Washington metro region is blessed to be an area where unemployment is lower than other regions of the country. There are a total of 140,072 businesses in the region, with an annual payroll of $134,509.7 million. This annual payroll is disbursed to 2,397,777 employees.[38]

With the recent economic downturn, more people looking for work have moved here for opportunities. Likewise, more businesses consistently move here for various reasons, including a more educated, skilled workforce and accessibility, especially as it relates to federal government contracts. It is prudent for our church to keep watch on these statistics and react to the nuances for various reasons, one being the evangelistic opportunity to reach out to new families moving to the area. Another compelling reason is that the DOT Model locates ministry opportunities close to where people live, work, or attend school in a manner that is mobile, accessible, proximate, and time-efficient and brings ministry to them.

EMPLOYMENT: DRIVE TIME AND MODE OF TRANSPORTATION

In the year 2010, there were 4,428,059 people who were sixteen years or over in the Washington metro area. Of this total, 3,244,659 were in the labor force (73.3 percent), and 1,183,400 were not (26.7 percent). For those still in the workforce 2,944,846 were working civilian jobs, 52,187 were in the armed forces and 247,626 were unemployed.[39] The commuting time for those that work outside the home varied, but for

1,559,096 people (55.9 percent), it was thirty minutes or more. Of this total, those with over one hour and one and a half hour commutes represented 351,094 and 117,658 individuals, respectively.[40]

The statistics show that the mode of transportation chosen by most was a car, truck, or van, with over 2,232,193 electing this option. People who drove alone or carpooled represented 65.6 percent and 10.6 percent, respectfully. Those who elected to take public transportation to work totaled 409,911, and other modalities accounted for 146,098.[41]

Later in this chapter, I will look at traffic congestion and its impact, which will give the reader a more informed picture of the commuter landscape. The statistical information gathered has significant concern for this church. How long a commute is and what mode of transportation impact the church in scheduling, attendance, finances, nurturing of relationships, and the frame of mind of parishioners in this urban ministry context. Data collected for your city in this area will have an impact on your church too.

The demographics presented in this section are not designed to bore the reader with statistical information about Washington, DC. The purpose is to demonstrate how this information can assist you, your church, and denomination in understanding your regional context for ministry. It is not only important for meeting the needs of the present community, but the data assists those who utilize it to be proactive as you plan for the future. Many of these statistical indicators justify the creation of a transportation-based network of small groups and the benefits derived from such a system.

SOCIAL NETWORKING: A MELTDOWN FOR A MELTING POT

There are 5.5 million stories to be told and heard in the National Capital Area. In this chapter, the demographics of the region have been presented in various forms, and it can be derived from these statistics that our church environment is a melting pot. The stories that need to be told and heard are urban and represent diversity. Whether you live in rural or urban areas of the world, the stories in your location need to be told as well. The church should be one of those places where these stories can be facilitated.

Washington, as most cities, is challenged by the urban infrastructure in which people do not know or care to know who lives next door. Neighborhoods, schools, and the location and attendees of churches are, by and large, geographically ethnic, limiting the opportunity for people to tell their own story or hear someone else's. Some do not know how to go about connecting with others or are fearful to reach out and trust so they can tell their stories. In chapter 1, isolation and fragmentation that exist in cities were explored. The challenge in this ministry setting was to promote an environment where people of all backgrounds could come and share their stories and faith.

Washington Beltway Community Church desires to facilitate the conversation so that the stories of many people can be told, heard, and, most importantly, shared. Every church has a responsibility to give voice to their congregations. This congregation has created the necessary environment for people to come from all walks of life, tell their stories, listen to the stories of others, and experience social networking.

Social networking has become a popularized term in the last few years with the innovation of modern technology, especially with the use of the Internet. Myspace, Facebook, Twitter, LinkedIn, and Meetup are all popular websites where millions go to reconnect with old friends, meet new friends, share their message or product, enroll in volunteer causes, and let people know what is on their mind. Even the US presidential election campaign has tapped into the social networking phenomenon.

Robert Wuthnow talks about the value of the Internet to the religious sector in his book, *After the Baby Boomers*. He states, "In comparison, the opportunities provided by the Internet for congregations, denominational offices, and other religious organizations to reach constituents in new ways are profound."[42] While many of these social networking sites can be and are extremely useful for our church, the connotation holds broader meaning for our ministry in our urban context.

In the book, *Planting and Growing Urban Churches: From Dream to Reality*, edited by Harvie Conn, Robert Linthicum describes what Christian networking looks like in the city. He writes, "Urban Christian networking builds and maintains contacts which will enable those in that network to more effectively carry out ministry to the exploited, the lost, and the unchurched."[43] Our congregation not only wants to build contacts with people who are not Christian through social networking (whether these are derived through personal contacts on the job, school, or Internet), but after they become Christians, provide them the opportunity to carry out their ministry. This is accomplished through the social networking of the spiritual gifts (1 Cor. 12-14) and utilization of the ministry gifts in (Eph. 4:11-12). When members of the church are not allowed or encouraged to exercise their giftings, then stories are not told, heard, or shared, and the flavor of the congregation is bland.

TRAFFIC CONGESTION AND ITS IMPACT: THE RIGHT OF PASSAGE TO GRIDLOCK

In the United States, driving is a privilege granted by state governments and administered by the Department of Motor Vehicles in the state where one lives. For most teenagers who reach the legislated age to drive and are issued a driver's license, it is a rite of passage to young adulthood, more independence, and responsibility. In many areas of the country, the "right of passage" connotes something entirely different—traveling to one's destination without major traffic jams and the right and opportunity to pass those who might be driving more slowly.

In our Washington, DC, ministry setting, as perhaps yours, the right of passage has become gridlock. This is true during normal rush-hour commutes as well as on weekends. We even have a traffic columnist writing for the *Washington Post* called "Dr. Gridlock," who reports on the traffic problem in the Metropolitan Region. It is noteworthy to repeat what was written in the Introduction, and that is that Washington has earned the infamous distinction of being in first place as the most traffic-congested city in the United States based on annual delay wasted hours per traveler.[44]

For the purposes of this book, the root causes of traffic congestion are explored to specifically provide some statistics that pertain to the Washington, DC, metropolitan region. It is this data that lends itself to the creation of the DOT Small Group (Cell) Model. In 2005, the US Department of Transportation Federal Highway Administration, Office of Operations, issued a report entitled *Traffic Congestion and Reliability: Trends and Advanced Strategies for Congestion Migration.* This report detailed the seven root causes of traffic congestion, which are traffic incidents, work zones, weather, fluctuations in normal traffic, special events, traffic control devices, and physical bottlenecks.[45]

This same report listed the top twenty-four traffic bottlenecks in the United States. The Washington, DC, metropolitan area made this list twice. Both of these locations are at junctions where I-495 (Capital Beltway) meets with other interstates. The first location is at the junction of I-495 and I-270 in Montgomery County, Maryland. This intersection is ranked seventh in the nation, with 19,429,000 annual hours of delays. The second location is at the junction of I-495 and I-95 in Prince George's County, Maryland, and is ranked fifteenth in the nation and attributed with 15,035,000 annual hours of delays.[46]

A more recent survey suggests that these two locations rank number three (I-495 and I-270—243,425 cars daily) and eleven (I-495 and I-95—185,125 cars daily) respectively for the worst bottlenecks in the nation. The Springfield, Virginia, interchange where I-395, I-95, and I-495 meet (also known as "The Mixing Bowl") was previously ranked fifth worst in the nation, but recent improvements have taken it off the top twenty list.[47] However, according to the Virginia Department of Transportation, the Springfield interchange carries more automobile volume with 430,000 cars daily.[48]

Multiple governmental jurisdictions, including federal and state governments, are attempting to combat the ever-increasing traffic problem. Government is not alone in combating urban traffic congestion, as many businesses have addressed the difficulty of employee mobility in the Washington metro region, which has an enormous productivity and economic impact. To lessen the burden on both employer and employee, businesses have combated gridlock by instituting flextime, telecommuting, and shorter workweeks. Unfortunately, the Church has not followed the government and private sectors in capitalizing on strategic planning in this area, to the detriment of the quality of the spiritual life of the believer and of those who might be won in the harvest. The Church must rise to the occasion and provide creative ideas to combat traffic congestion for their commuting members.

NEW WINESKINS FOR THE NEW WINE: GOING FROM GRIDLOCK TO GOD-LOCK

Jesus, the master storyteller, told the disciples a parable about wineskins and wine that is significant and as relevant today as it was then. His words recorded in the Gospel of Luke 5:37-38 say: "And no one puts new wine into old wineskins; otherwise the new wine will burst the skins and will be spilled, and the skins destroyed. But new wine must be put into fresh wineskins." In his book, *The Problem of WineSkins: Church Structure in a Technological Age,* Howard Snyder provides some insight and analysis of this passage. He writes:

> Jesus distinguishes here between something essential and primary (the wine) and something secondary but also necessary and useful (the wineskins). Wineskins would be superfluous without the wine they were meant to hold.
>
> This is vital for the everyday life of the church. There is that which is new and potent and essential—the gospel of Jesus Christ. And there is that which is secondary, subsidiary, man-made. These are the wineskins, and include traditions, structures, and patterns of doing things which have grown up around the gospel.... I am particularly concerned with the relationship between such wineskins and the gospel wine, and with the question of what kinds of wineskins are most compatible with the gospel in modern techno-urban society. For

> the wineskins are the point of contact between
> the wine and the world. They are determined
> both by the wine's properties and the world's
> pressures. Wineskins result when the divine
> gospel touches human culture.[49]

The Gospel of Jesus Christ (the message and new wine) never changes, but the methodology (the presentation and wineskins) must always evolve in the context of the world that we live in. Generally speaking, it is difficult for people to accept change as they become accustomed to their way of doing things, but change is really constant. God did not stop creating after day six of the creation narrative in the first chapter of Genesis. He continually creates and will still be creating in the last chapter of Revelation when He creates a new heaven and new earth.

Jesus has partnered with humankind in every generation since His resurrection to provide both the technology to facilitate our lives and the inspiration to utilize that technology to advance the Gospel. In many cases, He had the latter in mind, when the concept or idea was revealed. Looking at the last one hundred years, it can be seen that the inventions of the automobile, airplane, telephone, radio, television, and Internet have advanced the Gospel.

In the Washington, DC, context, as perhaps yours might be, one of our world's pressures is traffic gridlock, which has impacted the quality of life for everyone, including Christians who like to participate in church-related functions. Using Snyder's concept of wine and wineskins above, the properties of the new wine are able to confront our region's gridlock pressure and innovatively create a new wineskin. I am strongly convinced that the DOT Model is a transportation-based new wineskin for the new wine that will empower the creation and thriving of small group community for your church where people can meet God face-to-face, despite congested roadways.

The "how-to" of achieving community or executing a model to assist in arriving at that goal is not as important as understanding why the model and community are needed in the first place, as well as the underlying principles that support the model. A particular model is always adaptable and may become archaic as an old wineskin, but the principles of community are unchanging and live on as they have a biblical and theological foundation. Part Two of this book is devoted to exploring the theological foundations of community that articulate a small group theology as well as a transportation theology.

PART TWO: DISCOVERING THE THEOLOGICAL FOUNDATIONS

CHAPTER 3

SMALL GROUP AND
TRANSPORTATION THEOLOGY

Part 1 is dedicated to articulating the ministry context of your local church and the broader community in which it serves. As every house must have a solid foundation on which to build, so does your local assembly. The Apostle Paul declares in Ephesians 2:20 that the universal Church "has been built upon the foundation of the apostles and prophets, with Jesus Christ himself as the cornerstone." While this is absolutely true in a broad brushstroke approach, the details of foundation-building are seldom examined, understood, and expressed.

One of the main ingredients of apostolic and prophetic building is the concept of community, both in small groups and larger corporate worship. In order for any congregation to build upon this idea, one must be able to understand, model, and convey the vision of community to the church in a profound manner that embraces church philosophy and theology, which is the focus of Part Two of this book. This chapter takes a look at small groups and transportation theology, while the next provides the biblical justifications for small groups and transportation.

COMMUNITAS, ISOLATION, AND ALONENESS

The key to understanding any discipline is usually defining vocabulary appropriate to the subject matter. This is especially true when it pertains to theological fundamentals of community, isolation, and aloneness, which are important terms to the readers of this book. Community is defined by noted theologian Stanley J. Grenz in his book, *Renewing the Center: Evangelical Theology in a Post-Theological Era*: "[Community is] persons in relationship and is the central organizing concept of theological construction, the theme around which a systematic theology is structured."[50] For the church, it means that they participate in the lives of one another on an ongoing basis. This is especially important in an urban area, such as Washington, DC. Sometimes the intimate community (*gemeinschaft*) is misconstrued to be the society at large (*gesellschaft*). Mark Lau Branson discusses this in Craig Van Gelder's book, *The Missional Church in Context: Helping Congregations Develop Contextual Ministry*. He writes:

Cardinal Avery Dulles notes that Charles Cooley proposed a similar construct in his expansion of *gemeinschaft*. Dulles summarizes the characteristics of "primary groups": face-to-face association, the unspecified character of that association, relative permanence, the small number of persons involved, [and] the relative intimacy among the participants. I believe these characteristics help with my definition of community: a community is not a society; it is smaller, the shared meanings are more complex, its meanings and practices may or may not serve the purposes of the society, and the individuals are covenanted into the community so that they project themselves fully into the meanings and practices.[51]

The Latin word *communitas* encompasses a broader definition of community, which conveys an intense sense of togetherness rooted in something shared by participants through a rite of passage.[52] For the Christian, entrance into community is shared through the rite of passage of accepting Christ and being baptized into His body. Community is strengthened and fortified through Christian formation. The formation of Christian community is woven through the theological texts of the Bible from the creation of humanity in Genesis to the recipients of eternal life in Revelation. It is, therefore, important for the Church at large and specifically your local congregation to promote and foster real community for your members and those that reside in the larger community where you live.

If community is a shared sense of togetherness in experiencing life, then isolation is the opposite of community. Isolation can be defined as solitude, withdrawal, or not desiring to become a part of a vibrant community where others participate in that community. In the North American context, isolationism can be traced to the Enlightenment, as Darrell Guder explains in his book, *Missional Church: A Vision for the Sending of the Church in North America*. He writes, "A primary goal of the Enlightenment was to formulate a new basis of individual identity as the key to personal freedom."[53]

The concept of isolationism is wide-spread in our culture, affecting every segment of our society, including the way we live, work, and worship. The penetration of isolationism into the Church can be witnessed in how the church conducts worship in which people come as individuals and many times leave as individuals, rather than engrafted into a caring community. Those who are not part of a loving community find themselves experiencing aloneness.

Aloneness is the result or consequence of isolation, whether self-inflicted or not. Aloneness is counter-intuitive to the way we were created. Humans were created for intimate fellowship with each other and with God. Gareth Icenogle speaks to aloneness as not being the will of God in his book, *Biblical Foundations for Small Group Ministry: An Integrational Approach.* He writes, "We know that 'aloneness' is not a good state for humanity. Aloneness is not God's desire for men and women."[54] In the church context, a person can be a part of a mega-church of thousands but still experience aloneness if he or she is not in relationship with others. Through the lens of history and Scripture, one sees that God, humanity, and the Church were to be in a relationship, each within itself as a unit in each distinctive category and also with one another.

GOD IN RELATIONSHIP

God as creator of the universe could have chosen to exist by Himself, without experiencing isolation or aloneness as humans do. However, in His divine plan, the choice was made to include others and partner with them in relationships, providing the ultimate theological foundation of modeling and expressing community. I will now examine God in relationship as a small group, with angelic hosts, and with humanity.

AS A SMALL GROUP

This book is about small groups, and, as such, no better church or theological example depicting small groups can be articulated than God. Bill Donahue conveys this thought in the book, *Building a Church of Small Groups: A Place Where Nobody Stands Alone.* He writes: "You cannot come to understand the true nature of God unless and until you accept that he is not simply an individual. God is, in every sense of the word, a 'group' as well....Without an ounce of sacrilege, we might call the Godhead the first small group."[55] Each member of the Godhead is in relationship with one another—separate, distinct, and mutually permeating one another.

This is a prime example what the members of the small groups of our congregations should strive for. We should maintain the uniqueness of our individuality while at the same time blending our uniqueness with one another in very transparent ways. God does not only reveal His desire for community with Himself, but He also is in a relationship with angels and humanity.

WITH ANGELIC HOST

In the scholastic work, *The Anchor Bible Dictionary*, angels are described as heavenly beings whose function it is to serve God and to execute God's will.[56] Angels were created by God with free will. They are referred to in the sacred Scriptures as Sons of God, Holy Ones, Hosts, Army, agents, and messengers.

God partnered with angels in relationship to carry out divine tasks. Some of the tasks that angels performed were announcing the birth of Jesus to Joseph (Matt. 1:20), protecting Israel (Deut. 32:8), and ministering to the divine Christ (Matt. 4:11). Angels are also tasked as being guardians of humanity (Heb. 1:14).

WITH HUMANITY

God, who is in relationship with God's self and angels, is also found to be in relationship with humanity from the beginning. Gareth Icenogle articulates this principle by stating:

> God is described as existing in divine community, in dialogue with other members of the God-self, an intracommunicating group who also created humanity to exist in group intra-communication. God created and addressed humanity as community with community, as group with group. The divine community has existed in intercommunity with human community from the beginning. Three areas of dialogue and community are established from the beginning: within (intra) God's group self, within (intra) the human group and between (inter) God's group and the human group.[57]

If God is a proponent of relationships by modeling community with Himself, angels, and humanity, how much more should we be in relationship with one another?

HUMANITY IN RELATIONSHIP

God established the precedent for being a part of a community in relationality. He desires that humans also participate in the relational task by having meaningful interaction that fosters community with one another. This section will explore the types of relationships that humans have by looking at friendships, family ties, being part of a larger urban community, relating personally with God, and relating with the corporate Church.

FRIENDSHIP

It has been said that a dog is a man's best friend. While a dog's loyalty and love for its owner cannot be questioned, there is something about intimate friendships with other humans that cannot be replaced. This is because we are of the same species, made in the image and likeness of God. This likeness was so apparent that Abraham was called the friend of God (James 2:23). There are some friends that can transcend family ties and are closer than brothers (Prov. 18:24, KJV), such as Jonathan and David, whose souls were bound together (1 Sam. 18:1).

The small group is the ideal setting to experience community because it promotes the kind of relationships that only friends can have. This is where transparency, edification, accountability, acceptance, and transformation can take place in a loving atmosphere. Bill Donahue and Russ Robinson add the value and importance of friendships in the small group structure. They write:

The Bible presents yet another piece of socio-
logical evidence for community. It says that
we need friends to hold us accountable and
offer acceptance while we change. Friendships
can provide unique opportunities for spiritual growth, especially when we covenant to
be mutually vulnerable and tell the truth....
Proverbs 27:17 reminds us why we need fellowship for true spiritual growth: "As iron sharpens iron, a friend sharpens a friend" (NLT)....
Though most people have become resigned
to isolation, no longer expecting to find true
community, the church can offer ultimate
friendship.[58]

We have witnessed in our assembly in Washington
that small groups facilitate friendships, where bonds
have developed and life is shared outside the functions
of the congregation. This can be true for your church
where you live as well.

FAMILY TIES

The importance of families in human relationships
should not be underestimated. God designed that,
from the beginning, each of us should be birthed into
a natural family that provides care, nurturing, protec-
tion, and training so that we become mature adults.
Most people do not have a choice in the matter of what
family they are placed in. The first family consisted of
Adam, Eve, and God, and they were in relationship

as a small group and in community. Gareth Icenogle alludes to this when writing: "The human community exists foundationally as *small group*, that is, at least one man and one woman in relationship with God. Three persons were together in the Garden 'in the cool of the day' (Gen 3:8). The foundational theological community is man, woman, and God together."[59]

The concept of family is often used metaphorically by the Apostle Paul to describe the Church of Jesus Christ, where God is heavenly Father and we have identity as His children. Robert Banks alludes to this in his book, *Paul's Idea of Community,* when he writes, "All Paul's 'family' terminology has its basis in the relationship that exists between Christ, and the Christian as a corollary, and God. Christians are to see themselves as members of a divine family.[60]

To view your local assembly as a divine family, you should not look through the lens of the Western individualistic culture, which has been the frame of reference for many of us. The family must be understood in the context of the cultural setting of Jesus and the New Testament Church, which was group-oriented and not self-centered. When comprehending the importance of familial dynamics, only then can the application be transferred to the Christian family. Joseph H. Hellerman provides insight to the group-oriented mentality of the Mediterranean society and the Church in his book, *When the Church Was a Family: Recapturing Jesus's Vision for Authentic Community*:

> The New Testament church was decidedly strong-group in its social orientation, but this was no accident of cultural accommodation. Jesus unequivocally affirmed such an approach to interpersonal relationships when He chose "family" as the defining metaphor to describe His followers.... One's family demanded the highest commitment of undivided loyalty, relational solidarity, and personal sacrifice of any social entity in Jesus's strong-group Mediterranean world. And major life decisions were made in the context of the family.... So we should not be surprised to discover that for the early Christians, the overall health and honor of the church family took priority over their individual needs and desires. The same should be true of us.[61]

Through the small group, the family of God cares for one another, protects one another, edifies one another, and equips one another in order that we can become mature spiritual adults. Our congregation in Washington has witnessed these powerful dynamics of small group life, especially in our recovery groups where broken lives are being mended, hope restored, and a vision for their future reclaimed. The ties that bind both biological and spiritual families are relational in nature. Without authentic relationships, one may be part of a natural or church family but may not have closeness and intimacy with other members of the group.

AS AN URBAN COMMUNITY

The definition of family extends beyond the family of origin and the church family to encompass geographic places such as cities or countries. Questions of ethnicity, nationality, or the location of one's residence are common when getting acquainted with others. In the Old Testament, the twelve children of Jacob (Israel) became twelve tribes, and these tribes eventually became the nation of Israel. Author Ray Bakke, in his book, *A Theology as Big as the City*, dedicates one of his chapters to finding a theology of place in the Bible. Bakke writes:

> Early in the twentieth century, H. Wheeler Robinson coined the expression "corporate solidarity" to describe what he saw as "the synthetic grasping of a totality" in the thought of ancient Israel.... The relationship of the family to the larger national context must be interpreted with respect to this solidarity as well. Thus, tribes come from families and combine to form a nation..... If a city is anything, at least in idealized form, it is an organic, dynamic series of relationships, interwoven in a common crucible.[62]

Every urban community has a corporate identity of interwoven relationships, and your city is no exception. Those that live in the Washington, DC, metropolitan area, whether they live in DC proper or suburban Maryland and Virginia, are called Washingtonians. Our identity is not only linked geographically but politically as well, functioning as the seat of national government. Other definers of an urban community can be architecture (e.g., White House, Washington Monument, and Jefferson Memorial) or a sports franchise (e.g., Washington Redskins, Wizards, Capitals, and Nationals). When a local sports franchise wins the championship, they win for the entire city and its residents. Can you begin to formulate the corporate identifiers in your particular city?

Ray Bakke writes about city solidarity and ministry applications and states, "If the Bible teaches that cities are important beyond the fact that they are collections of individuals, then our ministry in cities must be both public and private, personal and corporate."[63] Our churches must embrace our "theology of place" to be in relationship and ministry in our urban community. Ultimately, we know that, as the Apostle Paul wrote, "Our citizenship is in heaven" (Phil. 3:20), but he was also a citizen of Tarsus (Acts 21:39). Our congregations must not forsake our citizenship, identity, and ministry on earth for the future when we become citizens in heaven.

WITH GOD

Earlier in this chapter, God's relationship with humanity was discussed. Inevitably, communication is a two-way street; not only does God want to have a relationship with us, but He desires that we have a relationship with Him. One of the spiritual disciplines that enables us to communicate and have a relationship with God is talking with Him in prayer. Jesus was our prime example, as He communicated with the Father in prayer in a personal way; however, He also advocated and participated in corporate prayer with the disciples.

When each of the individual members of the church has a personal intimate relationship with God, then once they gather together as a group, they can have intimacy with God and with each other. Gareth Icenogle conveys this thought when he writes, "Intimacy between group members pours out of intimacy with God. If the group can invest energy to be in God's presence, the hunger to experience one another's presence is not far behind."[64] Joel Comiskey shares the importance of prayer in the small group when he states, "A Spirit-filled group prioritizes prayer. Prayer is the life-breath and atmosphere of effective groups."[65]

AS A CHURCH

Humanity in relationship with one another and corporately with God can ultimately be expressed in community as both the local church and the Church universal. In his book *Liberating the Church: The Ecology of Church and Kingdom*, Howard Snyder defines the church community. He writes:

> The New Testament pictures the church as the community gathered around Jesus.... Matthew 18:20 is perhaps the most compact definition of the church in Scripture: "Where two or three come together in my name, there am I with them." What makes a church? One person is not enough. Even one person alone with Jesus ("just Jesus and me") is not the church. Church is community. Where two or three come together in Jesus' name, there church begins. The church is a community of people gathered around Jesus, committed to him, worshipping him, and ready to serve his Kingdom in the world. People gathered around Jesus is the irreducible minimum of the church.[66]

The Church is referred to as the body of Christ. Craig Van Gelder discusses the church as a network of human relationships with a spiritual purpose in his book, *The Essence of the Church: A Community Created by the Spirit*. He writes:

One of the most popular images for the church as a social community is the body of Christ. The image has functioned within the North American church in recent years to emphasize spiritual gifts and small groups. It was developed most fully by Paul.... The image of the human community as a body was a social-political idea current in Hellenistic circles in Paul's day. Paul reformulates this organic image by relating it to the crucified, resurrected, and ascended Christ.

The nature of the church entails a unity that transcends diversity. This unity is rooted in the sacrificial death of Christ and our common participation in this sacrifice. The church as the body of Christ is to live as a unified community in sacrificial love and fellowship. In relating this image to the resurrected Christ, Paul describes our being united in the body of Christ as the work of the Spirit, creating a new humanity. This new humanity functions as the body of Christ on earth under Christ's headship through the ongoing work of the Spirit who gifts, guides, and graces the church.... The church as the body of Christ is to live as a new community in dynamic, gift-shaped interdependence.[67]

While the body of Christ is expressed on a universal level, your local congregation is part of that larger body. At the same time, your assembly functions as a "body within a body," where people live in community and share their gifts with one another.

THE CHURCH AS A COMMUNITY WITHIN THE COMMUNITY: PARTNERING OF DIVINITY AND HUMANITY

In the last section, I noted that the church is comprised of gifted individuals in interdependent relationship with one another as a community. Your local assembly is situated in the larger context of a geographical community, in which life is to be lived and ministry performed. In order for the local church made up of human believers to be effective, there must be a mutual partnership between God and the believers. This partnering takes place in the congregation in belonging, gathering, sharing, and mission.

EKKLESIA

The word *church* (assembly or congregation) originates from the Greek preposition *ek*, "out of," and *klesis*, "a calling" (*kaleo*, "to call"). It was used among the Greeks of a body of citizens "gathered" to discuss the affairs of state.[68] The modern-day usage of *church* means those who are "called out." Peter talks about this concept as being called out of darkness into God's marvelous light (1 Pet. 2:9).

The Church is both local and universal in scope. Howard Snyder conveys this point in his book, *The Community of the King*. He writes:

The local church is always part of the one, holy, apostolic, universal Church of Jesus Christ. It must be seen in this larger perspective to be rightly understood. In one sense the Church is fully present in each local community of believers, for Jesus Christ is there. But each local church also participates in the one people of God scattered throughout the world.[69]

Your church assembly is a local community within the larger community of the universal church. If the universal church is to take the Gospel to the world, then your local assembly must take the good news of the Gospel and tangible hope to the outlying geographic community in which it is located. This means that the church is a community within a community. Bill Easum and Dave Travis articulate the point in their book, *Beyond the Box: Innovative Churches that Work*. They write:

When a church views its ministry as a larger part of a whole within a community, yet still knows its specific vision in relation to other kingdom churches, then the time, talents, and treasures of that congregation turn 180 degrees. But that's not all. Such a view of the church will not only change the way our local congregations function, but it will also change the way the unbelieving world thinks about the church.[70]

The church in Washington where I serve is attempting to be innovative and have a "beyond-the-box" presence in our community. We are doing this by bringing the church to the people, instead of the people going to the church building. It is a taking-it-to-the-streets approach. Our small group Bible studies and recovery cells meet in various venues in the marketplace, where we are easily accessible by mainstream society by various modes of transportation. How might you begin to think differently about your church's role and ministry to the greater community?

BELONGING

Belonging indicates identification with someone, someplace, or something. In most cases, people like to have a sense of belonging. For instance, we belong to families, schools, places of employment and we categorize our belonging by associating ourselves with the name of the entity we belong to. As Christians, we belong to the church, and the church belongs to Christ.

There are others who desire a sense of belonging whom God is "calling out" to be part of His Church. When a person experiences the saving power of Christ, that person automatically belongs to Him and the Church. Those who are born into the family of God should be welcomed and should feel as if they belong to the community of believers.

GATHERING

Those who belong to the *ekklesia* are commanded in the sacred Scriptures to gather together. Hebrew 10:25 is a prime text of the command to gather, which urges: "not neglecting to meet together, as is the habit of some, but encouraging one another, and all the more as you see the Day approaching." Gathering is foundational to community.

The members of the first-century church gathered together in small groups in the house and in larger groups in the temple (Acts 2:46-47). In the book *The Second Reformation: Reshaping the Church for the 21st Century*, William Beckham refers to this as the two-wing church. He writes: "The Creator once created a church with two wings: one wing was for large group celebration, the other wing was for small group community. Using both wings, the church could soar high into the heavens, entering His presence, and do His will over all the earth."[71]

Any congregation that adopts the two-wing approach will have celebration services and small group gatherings, where both wings are promoted by emphasizing the importance of attending celebration in small group gatherings and the necessity of being a part of small groups in the celebration service. This can be done through announcements and distribution of flyers at both functions. The criticality of both wings of community is most effective when visually demonstrated in the celebration service. In the church where I pastor, we place two eight-foot banners on each side of the podium, one which reads "Community: Small Groups" and the other reads "Community: Celebration." I explain the significance of these banners during the celebration service, which reinforces our desire to see people get connected and plugged in.

With modern technology, one can view church services on the television or Internet. While this is good use of something that God has given us (especially for shut-ins), it does not replace the concept of physically gathering together. In gathering, there is interaction and fellowship with God and one another.

KOINONIA

David Hesselgrave, in his book *Planting Churches Cross-Culturally: North America and Beyond*, provides a working definition of *koinonia*. He states, "*Koinonia* is usually translated 'fellowship,' but it could be justifiably translated 'joint participation' or 'partnership' (among other possibilities)."[72] Gathering together is not enough, but those that gather together must participate in partnership together. It is possible for people who come to church to be spectators rather than participants, sometimes by choice. Unless a mechanism is in place (e.g., small groups), it is easy to get lost in the crowd and not assimilated into the community life of the church. Being the church, belonging to the local assembly, gathering together, and participating together are not enough in the overall understanding of what the church is and does. There must be a goal of mission.

MISSION

While *koininia* denotes the healthy aspect of fellowship or participation in the church, the term *koininitis* (a play on *koininia*) has been used by others to identify the disease of too much fellowship or the inward maintenance focus of the church and little or no emphasis on outreach and mission. Missions are often confused with the concept of mission. In short, missions were viewed as an external outreach of the local church, where members supported the work that others were doing somewhere else. It was a kind of "I gave at the office" approach and I have done my part. While God desires for us to support missions outside of our churches, He has also given each of us "a mission" in the church where we actively participate in using our gifts to bless the church and community. M. Scott Boren discusses the distinction in his book, *Making Cell Groups Work: Navigating the Transformation to a Cell-Based Church*. He states:

The church at the center of society (Christendom) practiced the principle of missions, which involved missions giving, missions trips, missions reporting, and missionary commissioning. Missions were an activity that special people did in places outside of Christendom. Local churches supported these mission activities, but they were seen as something separate and ancillary from the general activities of the local church.... The church has realized that mission is something that is integrally tied to the meaning of being church in this world. The church is not the sending agency, it is the sent agency.[73]

The Great Commission was given to further the kingdom of God by making disciples in our world. In the book, *The Church of Irresistible Influence,* the authors provide advice on how to do this in any ministry context. They write:

If we are to succeed in our mission to further God's kingdom on earth, we must gather information that allows us to see our communities as they really are, and not merely as they appear to be.... Pastors don't need to become experts in sociology and anthropology; what they need to do is develop the skills of walking into a community setting and analyzing that setting to figure out what is going on there. Contextual analysis includes demographics, understanding the power structures of a community, understanding the economic base, and understanding what gives the particular ethos of that community.[74]

In the contextual analysis of the Metro Washington region, I recommended, and our church determined that transportation-based small groups must be a part of the equation for facilitating community and mission. The next section looks at transportation theology that will support my claims. Hopefully, this section will serve as one of the factors that will provide insight for you and your church to create a strategy for a transportation-based network of small groups.

TRANSPORTATION THEOLOGY AND THE CHURCH: FACILITATING COMMUNITY

For the church to gather, fellowship, and be engaged in mission, there must be a conscious or subconscious theology of transportation on the part of the church or people. This might entail choosing the physical meeting location of the church building, or, for the church member, what mode of transportation to utilize in order to attend. The early first-century Church embraced a theology of transportation, which will be discussed in this section. This segment also looks at the physical isolation and fragmentation that transportation theology can bridge, the modalities of transportation, as well as the difficulties encountered and the time spent in the endeavor.

ISOLATION AND FRAGMENTATION

Jesus preached in the country and in urban areas. The Church started in Jerusalem, an urban area, where people traveled from the countryside to the annual Feast of Pentecost. Since the beginning of the Church, travel has facilitated community and mission in both cities and rural communities and from suburbia to Urbana. Without transportation, people would be isolated and fragmented in a physical way, rather than the emotional or relational way that was conveyed earlier in the book. Wayne Meeks discusses the importance of mobility in the first-century Church in his book, *The First Urban Christians: The Social World of the Apostle Paul*. He writes:

> The guiding thread for every history of earliest Christianity, writes Martin Hengel, is the irresistible expansion of the Christian Faith in the Mediterranean region during the first 120 years. That expansion was closely associated with personal mobility, both physical and social.... Some of this travel was undertaken for the Christian mission, but much of the mission was carried out by people who were traveling for other reasons. Both were possible, and not surprising to the writers of the New Testament, because the people of the Roman Empire traveled more extensively and more easily than anyone before them—or would again until the nineteenth century.[75]

GETTING FROM HERE TO THERE

Personal mobility played a big role in establishing and maintaining community in the first-century Church. It has been calculated from the schematic itineraries of the Apostle Paul recorded in Acts that he traveled nearly ten thousand miles.[76] The travels of Paul and others were facilitated by a transportation infrastructure that allowed them to get from one place to another by land and by sea.

Wayne Meeks credits the Roman government infrastructure in the facilitation of travel of the first-century population. He states: "Roman power made possible this flourishing travel in two very practical ways: the Roman military presence undertook to keep brigandage on land and piracy on the sea at a minimum, and the imperial government took responsibility for a road system throughout its regions."[77] In your city and regions, the transportation infrastructure has made it feasible to utilize the various types of transportation for communal and missional experience for each local assembly. Automobiles and interstates and trains and rails have replaced mules, horses, and carriages in transportation theology. However, traveling and commuting does not come without its problems.

URBANIZATION AND
CRIPPLED COMMUTING

During Paul's time, travel presented its problems. Although Rome took responsibility for the road system, they still had to make road repairs. Those that traveled the roads were people of all different types, including the sick, fugitives, and prisoners. Traveling by sea could be risky, as storms would often materialize during the dangerous winter season from mid-November until early March.[78] Paul experienced shipwreck himself in Acts 28.

In most urban ministry contexts in the world, travel presents a problem too. Not only are road repairs necessary, but sometimes they aggravate an already congested traffic system. Budget deficits have also impacted needed improvements to road and rail systems. Most of all, travel has been impacted by the time that it takes to go from here to there.

ARE WE THERE YET?

When traveling with small children, a common question that may be asked is, "Are we there yet?" A comedy movie was made in 2005 using this same title. If the reply to that question is no, then the follow-up may be, "When are we going to get there?" This is because the time span for children to be still is considerably less than that for adults. When adults ask these same questions regarding travel time, it is usually because unforeseen circumstances await (construction, traffic accident, medical emergency, etc).

During the first century, Christians attempted to make good use of their time when traveling if they could afford it financially. Wayne Meeks conveys this in writing:

> The thriving maritime commerce was no less important for the early Christians' mobility.... Travel by sea was faster and cheaper than by land. Charlesworth estimates that an ancient ship could make one hundred miles in a day. On the land the state post instituted by Augustus, imitating a Persian model, made from twenty-five to thirty miles a day, including stops at *mutationes* for fresh horses. Ordinarily travelers, who had to haggle over rentals of mules, horses, or carriages, took much longer. The vast majority, including most likely Paul and his associates, would walk, and that was slower still: perhaps fifteen or twenty miles a day at most.[79]

Washington is the most congested city in the United States, wasting more hours in commuting than every other major city. I am sure that many reading this book feel they have it bad too when it comes to traffic congestion and wasting hours in commuting time. "Are we there yet?" is a common cry not only in Washington but in Sydney, London, Paris, Houston, Tokyo, and wherever you live. This is generally true for all travelers, even those commuting to church. A theology of transportation must include time efficiency as one of its components, but addressing the problem might include asking ourselves, "Should there be here?"

SHOULD THERE BE HERE?

The Church started at Jerusalem with a multilingual experience, but, in short order, Antioch became the center of a multicultural Christian outreach to the Gentile world. Antioch was a cosmopolitan city, capital of the Roman province of Syria, and strategically located on major trade routes. Antioch is the place where the term Christian (Acts 11:26) was first used, although in a demeaning manner. Paul recognized the importance of the Jerusalem Church, but he understood the strategic possibilities for effectiveness in Antioch so much that he set up base there. Roger Greenway adds, "As for its impact upon the world, Antioch soon came to supersede Jerusalem, developing into the missionary headquarters of the first century."[80] In our city, as probably yours, people already refuse to take jobs in certain sectors of the metro region because of traffic and commuting problems. The relevant point for our assembly and the Washington Metropolitan setting is that instead of going "there" to church amidst urban congestion, using a crippled transportation system and wasting time in the process that could be used more efficiently, we desire to bring the church "here" to where people live, work, and go to school and do so in a time-efficient manner. Guess what? You can do the same where you live by God's grace.

Harvie Conn and Manuel Ortiz, authors of *Urban Ministry: The Kingdom, the City and the People of God,* discuss the reshaping of the church in cities within the context of the mega-church. They write:

> As noted before, population mobility shifts are reshaping connections between city, suburb and edge city in the United States. These demographic adjustments are affecting the church and its targeted context. The mega-church's center of ministry appears to be shifting from a local neighborhood to a larger and more regional area, neither urban nor suburban but metropolitan. Many express that broad regional focus by relocating either near to or directly on a major avenue and/or interstate interchange…. The community church has become a delocalized regional church. And the regional church, now defining its neighborhood not by space but how long it takes to get there by public or private transportation, becomes a mega-church.[81]

Our local assembly does not want to become a mega-church but has some similarities to and some differences with what Conn and Ortiz describe above.

We are a church with a regional focus, but the difference is, instead of having a centralized building in one place near the interstate, we have many places near interstates and rail stations where our regional small groups can meet. These venues put "localization" in the regional concept by having them strategically positioned where people live, work, and go to school. They can use both private and public transportation and arrive time-efficiently in six to ten minutes using the DOT Small Group (Cell) Model. Now that the foundation of small groups and transportation theology for community formation has been laid, in the next chapter the theological justifications for small groups and transportation will be explored.

CHAPTER 4

BIBLICAL JUSTIFICATION FOR SMALL GROUPS AND TRANSPORTATION

Some believe that church-related small groups, which have multiplied in many countries in the last fifty years, are a relatively new way to foster community. In reality, these small groups have existed since the Church was started in the first century. Prior to the establishment of the Church, small groups were used in a variety of contexts, many described in the Old Testament Scriptures. The larger context of the "Universal Church" is not a new concept that began with this statement of Jesus to Peter: "On this rock I will build my church, and the gates of Hades will not prevail against it" (Matt. 16:18). This chapter explores the biblical witness of small groups in the Old and New Testaments, as well as sociopolitical forerunners of the larger *ekklesia*, which establish precedent and justification for your assembly to be a church of small groups and to worship as a church in the larger context.

JETHRO PRINCIPLE TO MOSES

Exodus 18 presents the story of Jethro, priest of Midian, counseling his son-in-law Moses concerning the duties of judging (deciding disputes) among the people from morning to night. The text as recorded in Exodus 18:17, 21-23 reads:

> 17: "Moses's father-in-law said to him, What you are doing is not good. You will surely wear yourself out, both you and these people with you. For the task is too heavy for you; you cannot do it alone."

> 21: "You should also look for able men among the people, men who fear God, are trustworthy, and hate dishonest gain; set such men over them as officers over thousands, hundreds, fifties, and tens."

> 22: "Let them sit as judges for the people at all times; let them bring every important case to you, but decide every minor case themselves. So it will be easier for you, and they will bear the burden with you."

> 23: "If you do this, and God so commands you, then you will be able to endure, and all these people will go to their home in peace."

Through the lens of this text, I will suggest that small groups will prevent burnout, help develop leaders, provide empowerment for leaders, and result in multiplication.

PREVENT BURNOUT

Jethro realized that Moses was wearing himself out and facing burnout in the way he was performing all the tasks of ministry himself. Have you, or someone else, ever thought you were on this same track? Jethro's solution for Moses was to delegate authority to leaders who would oversee small groups. One of the common problems that professional clergy face today is that they are too busy working seventy-hour workweeks and carrying too many responsibilities. Reggie McNeal writes about the job description versatility of the senior pastor in his book, *The Present Future: Six Tough Questions for the Church*:

> The senior pastor of a multiple-hundred-member congregation now must be manager of the corporate culture, headhunter, personnel manager, strategic planner, fundraiser, expert communicator, chief vision developer and caster, ministry entrepreneur, spiritual guru, architectural consultant, plus whatever particular assistance or role the congregation needs at any given time.[82]

It is impossible for most ministers to do all of these tasks well because some of the items are not their strengths. A scenario as the one presented above can lead to clergy burnout with, in some cases, the clergy person leaving the ministry. In most cases, though, the clergy stays but is not happy. Reggie McNeal discusses this in his book, *Practicing Greatness: 7 Disciplines of Extraordinary Spiritual Leaders*:

> Most ministry burnout among spiritual leaders is not the exotic type (usually involving some egregious moral failure) that garners all the press and gossip. Instead, it is typically the common variety of burnout that results from leaders dealing day in and day out with stuff that brings them no energy and does not play to their talents. Eventually, leaders run out of emotional, psychological, and spiritual reserve. A strong sense of call or commitment of a highly developed sense of responsibility may keep the leader in place, but only a shell of the formerly vibrant person remains.[83]

Small groups afford the opportunity for over-worked pastors to delegate authority to leaders who can assist in shepherding the flock. This reduces the time that pastors work each week in providing pastoral care. They can reprioritize their agenda and hopefully have a quality of life, while allowing others to use their giftings and feel useful.

LEADERSHIP DEVELOPMENT
AND EMPOWERMENT

Jethro understood that, for Moses to avoid burnout, he would have to look for other leaders to whom he could delegate responsibilities. First, the leaders were to be selected that had certain qualifications; next, they would have to be trained in how to judge disputes. In our church of small groups, as well as it will be for your church, it is important that leadership be identified and trained to help the senior pastor carry out the collective responsibility of attending to the needs of the people.

Not only did Jethro advise Moses to select qualified personnel to assist him in attending to the people's needs, but he suggested that Moses grant them power to govern. The new leaders were to handle the minor cases and bring the more complex cases to Moses, freeing Moses up for his other duties, including teaching the collective group of people. I realize that for leadership to be executed effectively, our small group leaders must not only do the work but be empowered in making decisions pertaining to the groups they lead. Likewise, the senior pastor must be available to the leaders for situations that may be more complex and to help coach and mentor these leaders so they can eventually handle them. Are you beginning to realize how small groups led by trained leaders who have received your delegated authority might be able to help you?

MULTIPLICATION

Jethro went a step further in his advice to Moses. He not only gave him counsel on leadership development and delegation, but he gave him the structure with which to do it. This structure was having multiple groups of people, in denominations of thousands, hundreds, fifties, and tens, that the appointed leaders could govern. With the totality of Jethro's wisdom, Moses could use the same principles or adapt them as the nation of Israel grew larger. If Moses can make use of delegation strategy, surely we can.

As our church in Washington is a cell-based church, multiplication is implicit in the DNA of the church. This does not only relate to the small groups but to leaders and coaches as well. We take it a step further than most cell-churches, in that our church base should multiply by having multiple celebration centers and starting new churches. This multiplication not only will continually grow the numerical size and health of your church, but each church member will benefit as everyone's giftings are being utilized.

THE MINISTRY OF JESUS CHRIST

There was no greater proponent of small groups than Jesus. Gene A. Getz, author of *Sharpening the Focus of the Church*, quantifies the amount of time that Jesus spent with individuals, groups, and the larger multitude. According to Getz, Jesus spent 67.5 percent of his time with groups and 32.5 percent of His time with individuals. Out of the 67.5 percent of His time He spent with groups, 25.2 percent was with larger groups (9.7 percent with multitudes and 15.5 percent with the larger group of disciples).[84] This would mean that Jesus spent 42.3 percent of His time in small groups and 74.8 percent of His time with individuals and small groups. Three of the prime groups that Jesus spent His time with were the twelve disciples, the three members of the inner circle of the twelve, and the larger group of seventy.

THE TWELVE DISCIPLES

Matthew lists the names of the twelve apostles in the Gospel bearing his name in chapter 10:

> 2: "These are the names of the twelve apostles: first Simon, also known as Peter, and his brother Andrew, James son of Zebedee, and his brother John;"

> 3: "Philip and Bartholomew; Thomas and Matthew the tax collector; James son of Alphaeus, and Thaddaeus;"

> 4: "Simon the Cananaean, and Judas Iscariot, the one who betrayed him."

Gene Getz, who provided the statistic that Jesus spent 67.5 percent of His time with groups, says that, in reality, he spent nearly 100 percent of His time with the Twelve. Getz explains:

> He, in a special way, spent His total time training these twelve men. Every time He spoke to the multitudes, the apostles had opportunity to hear what He said. Every time He healed a person, they could observe. Every time He dialogued and debated with the Pharisees, they looked on with amazement. In almost every instance when He talked with individuals, they also listened in – or at least got first hand feedback.[85]

Jesus had an infiltrating, vertical-down communication style: from crowd to core and from multitude to the larger body of disciples (seventy), to the Twelve, to three, and then to one. Getz states:

> Notice too the unique pattern that frequently emerged in Christ's overall ministry. At times He would be teaching the multitudes; then He would turn to the larger groups of disciples and speak to them more personally. And on occasion, He would turn to the Twelve and speak even more specifically and intimately about the truth He was teaching the larger group. Going a step further, He would at times turn to one individual or perhaps two or three of the Twelve to share with them some truth even more forcefully.[86]

Jesus was demonstrating that He invested in the life of His leaders by spending large amounts of time training them, either alone, as a group, or in the presence of others. To be successful leaders, we must follow the example of Christ and invest a large portion of our time and energies training and developing leaders by being present with them. Have you ever thought about how you are spending large quantities of time in the ministry and with whom? Do you find yourself spending most of your time putting out fires or in meetings? To be successful as a leader, we can follow the example of Christ and invest a large portion of our time and energy training and developing leaders by being present with them.

THE INNER CIRCLE OF THREE

One account of the three in Jesus's inner circle is recorded in the mountaintop transfiguration narrative in Matthew 17:1. "Six days later, Jesus took with him Peter and James and his brother John and led them up a high mountain, by themselves." Peter, James, and John were the three disciples in Jesus's inner circle. James and John were brothers and the sons of Zebedee. It is interesting to note that, in the listing of the disciples in Matthew 10, Peter, James, and John are three of the first four disciples.

Jesus took Peter, James, and John aside from the rest of the twelve apostles on several occasions to share more intimate details. It was a small group within a small group, as the small groups are *ecclesiolae in ecclesia* (little churches within the church). They were chosen by Christ to be key leaders of the disciples and eventually the Church. Michael Mack writes about the relationship between Jesus and His inner circle in his book, *The Pocket Guide to Burnout-Free Small Group Leadership: How to Gather a Core Team and Lead from the Second Chair*. He writes:

> "The Best Small Group Leader Ever" formed a small team that would eventually change the world....Three of these men (Peter, James, and John) became Jesus' inner circle or what would be called his "core team." Jesus poured his life into these three men, investing into them and modeling a life surrendered to the Father for them. He took three away with him to pray and heal, and they were with him when he was transfigured. While Jesus did not ignore the other apostles or his followers, he focused on these three with extra time and attention. He intentionally discipled these three and developed them into leaders.[87]

When a few people are separated from the larger group, the purpose can be misconstrued by those separated from the larger group and by those remaining. Gareth Icenogle writes about the possibilities of misunderstanding and the greater purpose of the setting apart of Peter, James, and John.

> Jesus was willing to risk the divisive potential of taking three away from the Twelve to experience together a unique event. Many would argue that this could have been a disastrous leadership miscalculation. When a cohesive group is subdivided in experience and connectivity with the leader, the whole group is often thrown off balance. Group cohesion is a factor of mutual trust in a small group. If members of the same group are subdivided and led into diverse experiences, the subgroups are likely to become distrustful of one another. The inner group is perceived to have more influence with the leader and the outer group is perceived as having less power....Jesus risked this more intimate relationship with the inner group of three not to make them an *elite* above the Twelve, but to make them an *elect* for the Twelve and the many.[88]

Peter, James, and John were set apart for extensive teaching by Jesus and to be used as key leaders for the disciples and for the Church to be established. They were not to be the elite of the apostles but were to function as servants for the apostles. The key leaders that will arise in the local ministry context in your church and region must have the same heart for servanthood, and the senior pastor must prioritize time with these leaders to offer extensive teaching and training.

THE SEVENTY

Both the twelve disciples and the inner circle of three are identified by name. This is not the case of the seventy. However, the mission of the seventy was clear, as Luke articulates in his gospel: "After this the Lord appointed seventy others and sent them on ahead of him in pairs to every town and place where he himself intended to go" (Luke 10:1).

The seventy were the advance team of Jesus. They traveled to the towns where Jesus would soon arrive, taking nothing with them but looking for a person of peace to dwell with there. While there, they not only announced the coming of Jesus but were engaged in ministry of healing the sick and casting out demons. If the town was not receptive, they would shake the dust off their feet and move on to another town.

The ministry of Jesus Christ through the small groups of His inner circle, the Twelve, and the seventy have relevance in a pastor's or denominational leader's approach in leading and modeling a church of small groups. Bob Logan and Neil Cole translate the small group ministry of Jesus to contextualize modern-day ministry in *Beyond Church Planting, Pathways for Emerging Churches.* They write:

> The Twelve: The foundation stones or strategic transformers

The Three: The foundation builders or catalytic leaders

The Seventy: The lay leaders who provide strategic implementation[89]

The involvement of the senior pastor is the investment of time into the life of the lay leaders, more with the core leaders, and the most time with identified key leaders.

ANTECEDENTS OF EKKLESIA SMALL GROUPS

When some think of a Christian meeting place, they think of a church building, a sacred place that has stained glass windows, a steeple, pews, altar, choir loft, chandeliers, baptistery, carpet, offices, lobby, and central air-conditioning. The reality is that church buildings were not originally the place where worship was practiced in the first-century church, because they did not exist. Christians did not begin to build church buildings until about 200 CE[90] According to Bart Ehrman, "The earliest Christian church building to be uncovered by archaeologists (actually a house that was converted to serve as a church in the city of Dura in Eastern Syria) dates from around the year 250 CE, well over two centuries after the death of Jesus."[91] Earlier in this book, *ekklesia* was defined as a people who are "called out." In this section, a portrait will be provided of the forerunners of the modern-day church and its small groups by elaborating on households, voluntary associations, synagogue, and philosophic and rhetorical schools.

THE HOUSEHOLD

The community formation of the early first-century house-church resided in their *"Sitz im Leben"* (setting of life) in the Mediterranean culture. They saw life from a group perspective, not through the lenses of individuals as is practiced in western culture. Bruce Malina states, "Our first century person would perceive himself as a distinctive whole set in relation to other such wholes and set within a given social and natural background; every individual is perceived as embedded in some other, a sense of embeddedness, so to say."[92] Culturally, this was the very reason why whole households (*oikos*) would be added to the church.

Households were large, inclusive communities consisting not only of a principal family, but also of slaves and friends, tenants, and partners or clients who would have been involved in common commercial or agricultural enterprises.[93] It was these households that provided ideal meeting places for the early Christians.[94] The size of the house church was limited by the size of the largest room in the house, generally the dining room (which might open into a peristyle or portico). In western culture, such a house would be a status symbol, but Gerd Theissen states that, in the world of the first-century Christian, "Houses provided information about private circumstances rather than public status."[95]

The book review of *Families in the New Testament World: Households and House Churches* appeared in the April 1999 edition of *The Catholic Biblical Quarterly*. Carolyn Osiek and David Balch asked themselves "how the architectural patterns of Roman homes formed and influenced relationships in early Christian house-churches" and "how worship in these house-churches influenced Christian families." They believe that their study yields a "surprising result": early Christian writers, as a whole, were not interested in the family as a topic; they were interested rather in "family and household as image and proving ground for the church."[96] This is not the case in our society today, but perhaps if Christian families were to see their household units as an extension of the church, the purpose of mission would be engrained in the basic living environment.

The household was a hierarchical body under the authority of the father. Decisions would have been taken corporately, or more probably, by the leading member of the household on behalf of others, even in matters of Christian conversion and baptism. The household was ready-made to serve as the "basic cell" of the church and the primary unit for mission as it used its existing network of relationships outside its own membership to spread the Gospel.[97]

It appears that the Apostle Paul was well acquainted with the importance of the household in his evangelistic mission of the Gospel. Roger Gehring discusses the *oikos* formula strategy of Paul in his book, *House Church and Mission: The Importance of Household Structures in Early Christianity.* The formula is based on the conversion experiences of the entire households of Cornelius, Lydia, Titus, Stephanas, Gaius, Crispus, and the Jailer at Philippi.

> The *oikos* formula confirms therefore that it was typical of the Pauline missional approach in any given city to initially target individuals from higher social levels. In this way Paul was able to win homeowners, along with their entire households, for the gospel and to set up a base of operations in their house for local and regional mission. The baptism of entire households surely accelerated the spread of the gospel. Another positive aspect of this phenomenon is the corporate solidarity effective as a result of the conversion of an entire household at once. From the very beginning of one's spiritual journey, each individual experienced the built-in-

support of his or her decision for Christ in the rest of the newly converted household. Each new Christian was immediately integrated in a community of faith that provided significant assistance for further growth as a believer.[98]

VOLUNTARY ASSOCIATIONS

The Roman Empire had numerous clubs, guilds, and associations, some of which were secret and uncontrolled. Roman officials often associated Christian groups with this sort and thought they might be attempting to cause division or overthrow the government. The voluntary associations were small groups and similar to many of the Pauline small groups in structure. By the nature of their structure, voluntary associations were one of the precursors to the small group of the first-century Church. One benefit to belonging to a voluntary association was a type of modern-day burial insurance, where its members were buried at no cost to them or their families.

THE SYNAGOGUE

Jesus and Paul often went to the synagogue to read, speak, and discuss the sacred Scriptures. The structure of the Jewish synagogue had a requirement that there must be ten people for a synagogue to be established. There was an overlap of many of the practices of Judaism into Christianity, as worship was conducted not only in the synagogue, where many were members of voluntary associations, but also in the households. There was a sense of being at home in conducting Christian mission in both the synagogue and individual households.

PHILOSOPHIC AND RHETORICAL SCHOOLS

Numerous debates have sprung up over whether or not Paul himself founded a school, but Paul did teach and train disciples who were able to articulate the Gospel and defeat its opponents using apologetics, which means defense strategy. It is documented in Acts 19:9 that Paul debated in the School of Tyrannus, which Neil Cole suggests was probably a school of philosophy and discourse.[99] Many of these schools were structured similar to household and voluntary associations that were common throughout the culture. It appears that these predecessors of church small groups provide some nuances of similarity with the first-century Church, but there were also distinctions which are not explored in this section. In the next section, the small-group and large-group functionality in the life of the Church situated in the first century will be reviewed.

THE FIRST-CENTURY CHURCH

The Church founded in the first century illuminates the theological justification for transportation small groups within an urban context. In this segment, the infant Church is investigated in urban centers where transportation was utilized to commute to the small and large gatherings of worship. This exposé is not meant to be landmarkism (i.e., requirement to go back to the original landmark to be correct in our theology) but does provide a precedent, which can be viable in our modern-day ministry setting when adapted.

URBAN CENTERS

Cities were prime areas of purpose-driven evangelism for the Church in the first century. After all, Jerusalem was the birthplace of the Church, which was begun on the Day of Pentecost, circa 33 CE The city of Jerusalem had a population of about eighty thousand people at the time.[100] Urban Centers were ripe for presenting the Gospel of Jesus Christ, because of shared conveniences, definable characteristics, and large populations.

First-century cities had definable characteristics by which they were known, as many cities do today. Authors Harvie Conn and Manuel Ortiz note a few of them: "Tyre was a port city based on maritime monopoly; Ephesus, a major cosmopolitan center of the Hellenistic and Roman cultures, was the leading seaport of Asia Minor and its greatest commercial city in the days of Paul; and Damascus was an international trade and political center."[101] Many of the cities were destinations on the Apostle Paul's three missionary journeys. He wrote letters to churches located in cities such as Rome, Corinth, and Ephesus, to name a few.

As mentioned earlier, Antioch became the base for Paul's ministry outreach to the Gentiles. Antioch was truly a model for modern-day multicultural ministry. Ray Bakke discusses the ethnic makeup of the city and the leadership of the church who were reflective of their members.

> Finally, Luke's Pentecost story climaxes with the establishment of the Antioch church, the first city-center church.... The city, like the old city of Jerusalem today, was divided into Greek, Syrian, Jewish, Latin and African sectors with a population between 500,000 and 800,000 residents.
>
> Apparently, in Antioch, people of different ethnic backgrounds began to cross the interior walls of the city to hear the gospel and join the church. The Jerusalem church heard about this and sent Barnabas...and Barnabas built a pastoral team that consisted of Simeon the Black (an African), Lucius of Cyrene (A North African), Manean (possibly a slave of Herod's father), Saul of Tarsus (native of Asia Minor, the land bridge to Europe) and Barnabas himself (from Cyprus).
>
> So the first large city-center church we know anything about had a five-person pastoral team from three continents. In Jerusalem they spoke many languages; now in Antioch they were fleshing out multiculturalism in the structure

> of the pastoral team. For me the principle is
> profound: the local city church staff should
> increasingly match the ethnicity, class and cul-
> ture of the church's members.[102]

What is interesting in some modern-day, large multicultural churches is that the principle of multi-cultural leadership staffing at the highest levels is not adhered to. When this is not modeled on the pastoral plane in the local congregation, then philosophically real multiculturalism may be questionable and the possibility of other forms of exploitation (e.g., finan-cial or human resources) may exist. The first century had cities that were defined by their geography, indus-try, and diversity, and the believers in these communi-ties became members and leaders of the local church.

TRANSPORTATION

Transportation has always played a part in the life of the Church as travel is an essential role in the spread of Christianity. The Church of the first century did not have the modern-day conveniences of automobiles, subway trains, and buses. The methods of travel were walking, mules, horses (sometimes with carriages), and ships. Jesus, the founder of the Church, walked (John 7:1), rode a donkey (Matt. 21:7), and rode on a ship (Matt. 9:1) in order to perform ministry. James talked about the common practice of the art of riding a horse (James 3:3).

As mentioned in chapter 3 of this book, people of the time utilized the types of transportation that would get them to their destinations in the shortest amount of time, if financial resources would allow. When traveling by road, Paul and others took advantage of the public transportation infrastructure already in place, which was built by the Romans. *The Anchor Bible Dictionary* describes the Roman road system this way:

> All roads led to Rome in NT times…. The good workmanship put into Roman roads is evident from the survival of many of them to this day: They learned some road-making techniques from the Etruscans, but the idea of continuous paved roads was Roman. A road required a sound foundation, efficient drainage, and where necessary, strong bridges.[103]

As leaders and members of churches and denominations, we can view the transportation infrastructure theologically, as a means of performing ministry in an efficient manner in our modern-day ministry environment, as did the first-century Church in its setting. City planners in your area have already built the roads and laid the tracks that all lead to where you live, as they have here in Washington, DC. We have opted to use the transportation infrastructure to our advantage by positioning our small groups in locations that are mobile, accessible, proximate, and time-efficient. You too, may be able to capitalize on the transportation infrastructure in your region to position small groups for maximizing your ministry in the marketplace.

HOUSE CHURCHES

The early church met in the homes of its members. According to the authors of *Home Cell Groups and House Churches*, "The house-church emerged in the New Testament era and continued as the most pervasive form of church structure until the time of Constantine (312 CE). Church buildings then came into prominence, and house-churches became a minor expression of church life."[104]

In the New Testament, there are at least three instances of house churches. The first is in the home of Priscilla and Aquila, where Paul said, "Greet also the church in their house" (Rom. 16:5). Another reference to this church in the home of Priscilla and Aquila is found when Paul says, "The churches of Asia send greetings, Aquila and Prisca, together with the church in their house, greet you warmly in the Lord" (1 Cor. 16:19). The second mention is found when Paul sends greetings "to Nympha and the church in her house" (Col. 4:15). The last reference to house churches cited in this book is that of Philemon when Paul said, "To Philemon our dear friend and coworker, to Apphia our sister, to Archippus our fellow soldier, and to the church in your house" (Philem. 2). "On occasion, whole congregations in one city might be small enough to meet in the home of one of the church's members; and other times house-churches appear to have been smaller circles of fellowship within the larger group."[105] Robert and Julia Banks, authors of *The Church Comes Home*, provide some insight to the size of the gatherings in the house church. They write:

> Smaller and larger meetings took place in a house or apartment, rather than in a special building. Such groups were not very large. Considering the size of average first-century houses (which were owned by less than 20 percent of the population), there were probably twelve to fifteen persons meeting in "the church in the house" and no more than sixty to eighty as "the whole church."[106]

The New Testament Church clearly met in houses but also had a larger worship experience at the setting of the temple.

TEMPLE WORSHIP

The temple was the gathering place for larger assemblies, as it was a large building and a sacred place. The temple was a permanent structure that superseded the mobile tabernacle. There were three temples in Judeo-Christian religion: Solomon's, Zerubbabel's, and Herod's. Bart Ehrman says, "In the days of Jesus, the Temple complex encompassed an area roughly 500 yards by 325 yards, large enough, as one scholar has pointed out, to enclose twenty-five football fields."[107]

The early church worshipped in the temple as a corporate group, complementing the small group meetings of the house church (Acts 2:46). Peter and John went up to the temple at the hour of prayer (Acts 3:1); Paul was seized in the temple (Acts 26:21); and Jesus even went to the temple on numerous occasions, one in which he turned over the merchant tables as they sold to the crowd who gathered there (Matt. 21:12). Both the small group (house church) and larger group (temple) worship experience were important to the first-century Church. Most of these churches were in urban venues, similar to where your church may be located. The relevant question for today asks how we as leaders and members of churches and denominations may be mindful in linking the past to the future.

COMMUNITY OF MEMORY TO A COMMUNITY OF HOPE: LINKING PAST TO FUTURE

The first-century church forged community by meeting together in both small groups (house churches) and larger groups (temple worship). All of the local churches in existence today, including the church you lead or are a member of, is only a sliver of the continuation of the Church that was founded in the first century. Almost two thousand years have transpired from then to now, but the principles of community remain unchanged. In this section, I will discuss how to link the past of the early church to project the future of community expression in the church where you worship and serve.

THE WAY WE WERE

"Memories" was the first word of the lyrics in the soundtrack of the 1973 blockbuster movie *The Way We Were*. Barbara Streisand, who starred in the movie with Robert Redford, also was the vocalist for the soundtrack. Memories carry thoughts into the present and are derived from how things were in the past. In order for your church to minister in the present and future in community, you must remember the past, where the early church modeled community. Stanley Grenz provides insight into how to accomplish this.

> The role of any group as a community of reference is connected with its ability to forge a link both to the past and to the future, that is, with its ability to function as what Josiah Royce called a "community of memory" and a "community of hope." Every community has a history; in fact, it is in an important sense constituted by that history. This constitutive narrative begins "in the beginning," with the primal events that called the community into being. Rather than

forgetting its past, a community retells the story of its genesis and of the crucial milestones and struggles that have marked its subsequent trajectory. Recalling the narrative past places the contemporary community within the primal events that constituted their forebears as this particular community. By retelling the narrative, the community retries its past—i.e., brings the past into the present—and thereby the narrative reconstitutes the present participants as the contemporary embodiment of a communal tradition that spans the years.... The church is a community in this sense.[108]

Each individual assembly can recall the memory of the community of the past experienced in small groups of the first-century church by revisiting the narratives written in the sacred texts. These texts are communicated in the present to link the past with the community of hope that is desired in the future.

FUTURE SHOCK

Future Shock is a book written in 1970 by Alvin Toffler, which depicts that too much change in too short a period of time is overwhelming to most people.[109] This has proved not to be the case for society at large, as we look forward to the next innovative idea that can change our lives. Perhaps the real shock of the future is embedded in the writing of Reggie McNeal in his book, *The Present Future*.

> We think we are headed toward the future. The truth is, the future is headed toward us. And it's in a hurry (we now know the universe is speeding up, not slowing down). We also generally think that the present makes sense only in the light of the past. Again, we need to check our thinking. The present makes clearest sense in the light of the future. We humans write history by looking at the past. God creates history ahead of time. He never forecasts. God always backcasts. He began with the end in mind. The future is always incipient in the present.[110]

The reality for your church is that God has written your history, and the future is headed toward you instead of you going to it. This, though, does not mean that those who belong to your church should not be prayerful and seek the direction of God. While we may understand where we might be going to some extent, many times we are unsure of exactly how we are going to get there, and this is where God's guidance is mandatory.

Our future is heading toward us by invoking the past. We are going back to the future by fostering community as the first-century Church did through the dual meeting structure of small groups and large gatherings. There must be a bridge that links the community of memory of the past to the community of hope in the future.

BRIDGE TO SOMEWHERE

In the architectural realm, a bridge is an intermediate structure that spans space or water to connect at least two geographical points. The link or bridge from the past to the future is the immediate present. The future is heading back toward us, but our expectation for what the future holds projects from the present forward. The casting of the God-given vision that your church is to experience in the future must be told in light of the past and the present. Stanley Grenz explains:

> Rather than ending in the past, the narrative history extends into the future. By expectantly looking to the ideal or "eschatological" future when its purpose and goals, its *telos*, will be fully actualized, a community turns the gaze of its members toward the future.... By narrating an overarching, "cosmic" story that spans the ages, the community's constitutive narrative provides a transcendent vantage point for life in the present. The recited narrative provides the overarching plot through which members of the community can view their lives and the present moment in history as a part of a stream of time that transcends every particular "now."[111]

The bridge for your church is to express the vision for the future in the present, by linking your heritage and purpose to the past of the first-century Church. You will be declaring that throughout the ages of the Church, both small groups and corporate worship were to be a part of church history as a whole, and we participate in that history in the here and now. This book now transitions to Part Three, where I will share the vision by discussing the small group network and transportation network strategies and their implementation.

PART THREE: STRATEGY AND IMPLEMENTATION

CHAPTER 5

SMALL GROUP NETWORK STRATEGY

The Prophet Habakkuk wrote these words concerning the importance of casting the vision and putting it in writing: "Then the Lord answered me and said: Write the vision; make it plain on tablets, so that a runner may read it" (Hab. 2:2). In Part Three, I will share the transportation-based small group network vision for Washington Beltway Community Church (WBCC) in writing so that others may read it. The goal is for you as pastors, denominational leaders, and church members not only to read but catch the vision so that you too might run with it in your churches and cities located around the world.

As mentioned before, I do not desire you to, nor is it possible for you to, duplicate these methods exactly and be successful. This is because each church is unique, having its own church government, DNA, and geographic makeup. However, the Lord can use these concepts as a starting point to provide insight, breathing a fresh wind of innovation to adapt this type of strategy for your ministry context.

In chapter 5, the small-group network strategy will be discussed, which will elaborate on WBCC's small groups, new member assimilation, leadership development, celebration services, and grand celebration services. Chapter 6 will detail the transportation-based network strategy using the DOT Small Group (Cell) Model. Chapter 7 fuses the small group and transportation-based network strategies in implementation, while chapter 8 explores missionary training and the evaluation and continual improvement process of the DOT Model.

COMMUNITY GROUPS: GOOD THINGS COME IN SMALL PACKAGES

The expression "Good things come in small packages" is a cliché which indicates bigger is not always better. This is also true for the size of churches. Historically, church health has been judged on quantitative numerical size and not on factors that determine qualitative growth. The Natural Church Development Survey is the most comprehensive study ever conducted on the causes of church growth, with more than one thousand churches participating (thirty members from each church) from multiple denominations in thirty-two countries (eighteen languages) on six continents that has resulted in 4.2 million responses.[112]

Christian Schwarz discovered through the results of this survey that there are eight quality characteristics present in churches that are growing. One of these characteristics is holistic small groups that multiply. Schwarz goes on to say, "If we were to identify any one principle as the 'most important'—even though our research shows that the interplay of all basic elements is important—then without a doubt it would be the multiplication of small groups."[113]

Small groups in the life of the church are known by various titles, to name a few: *koinonia* groups, cell groups, transformational groups, life groups, and home fellowship groups. We have chosen to call our small groups "community groups," which is common in the small group movement. In this section, I will discuss the specifics of our community groups, which include function, frequency, size, types of groups, curriculum, and multiplication criteria.

FUNCTION AND FREQUENCY

WBCC's community groups follow the structure of the cell church. These groups meet weekly, away from the church campus where regular Sunday celebration services are held. Currently, our community groups are meeting in various locations throughout the Washington, DC, metropolitan region.

The community group in our setting accomplishes the following purposes. It serves as the primary vehicle for interpersonal relationships where people can love one another, be loved, and make friends. It is a place where pastoral care can be offered by the other members of the group, equipping and discipleship can be performed, and individual gifts can be exercised in body ministry. It is conducive to evangelism by inviting nonbelievers to a more relaxed and less intimidating place than a church building, with the ultimate goal of multiplication.

Again, the small community groups in our church are not an auxiliary or another department in the church, which has a designated minister overseeing small groups competing with other department heads for financial allocation and the time of the senior pastor. These small groups are the church. Many churches with small groups attempt to assimilate new converts from the Sunday morning services to the small groups or from crowd to core. In the cell church, this process is inverted, going from core to crowd or small group to celebration. This seems to be more effective for the personal growth and retention of the believer. In their book *The Small Group Book*, Dale Galloway and Kathi

Mills share their experience at New Hope Community Church, located in Portland, Oregon. They write:

> For a large percentage of our members, involvement in a small group is a given, because they come into the church through small-group ministry and are later assimilated into the weekend celebration services. This is a simpler and much more effective transition than trying to convince people whose church mindset consists of once a week on Sunday mornings to become involved in a small group experience. In fact, over the years we have observed that those who come into the church via Sunday morning services and do not subsequently become involved in small groups are the ones we ultimately lose. Why? Because they simply don't feel connected, cared for, or needed. The chances of these people moving into true discipleship are slim.[114]

I and our local assembly adopted the approach of making small groups the main gateway to the church. This way, new people can connect, belong, be cared for, and have the opportunity to get involved in an optimal-sized small group.

SIZE

Optimal size of a small group is usually stated in reference to the minimum and maximum number of people needed to maintain intimacy, participation, and cohesion in the group. This if often debated among scholars, sometimes vehemently, especially on the upper limit of the group. Richard Peace, professor at Fuller Theological Seminary, practitioner, and author of numerous books on small groups, adamantly recommends five to thirteen people.[115] Joel Comiskey, author, practitioner, and coach, defines the size as between three and fifteen individuals.[116] Cesar Castellanos, pastor of International Charismatic Mission in Bogota, Colombia, strictly follows the guidelines of the number of twelve for the cap on the members of a small group.[117] There are others who have also weighed in on this debate. In short, you will have to customize your small group structure to what best fits your church's individual setting.

The minimum-maximum numerical boundaries for the size of our small groups are three to ten. The maximum number of people in a cell group will be ten people, which is coincidentally the number of people that were required to constitute a synagogue in Jewish theology. The number ten was chosen, not out of any spiritual connectivity, but because it is a nice round number for mathematical calculation purposes, using a power of ten exponentially for multiplication planning. This can be seen in the illustration that follows, depicting our small group model, which includes small groups, celebrations, and grand celebrations.

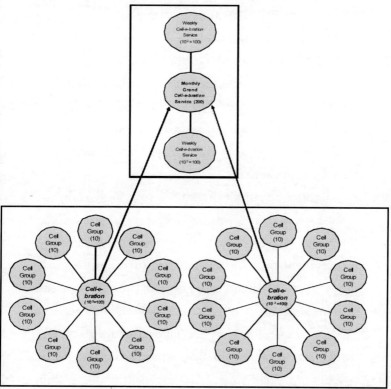

Figure 5.1 - WBCC small group model

TYPES

The vision for the types of small groups to be established is a long-range process. Currently, we are concentrating on developing a regional network of generic cells and recovery small groups. At the time of this writing, we have various small groups meeting in Alexandria, Arlington, and Springfield, Virginia, Washington, DC, and Bethesda, Maryland.

A generic cell is open to everyone, has a maximum of ten people, meets weekly in various locations in the metro region, has a standard teaching lesson, is evangelistic, and is expected to multiply when more than ten people are members of that cell. One synonym for a generic cell is "heterogeneous cell," and this is the most common type of small group. These generic cells have multiple benefits.

The first benefit is that, in these generic cells, the same topical lesson will be shared in all the cells in the region. Eventually, it will be our goal for the lesson segment of the generic cell to follow the Sunday morning celebration teaching, so that the message can be repetitive for maximum edification. The believer can hear the teaching on Sunday and know that it will be the lesson of the small group meeting that week. In between these times, the lesson can be digested, reflected upon, and studied in preparation for the small group discussion in which the participants will have a chance to share with each other.

The second benefit is that since the small group lesson is standard, believers can choose to belong to a small group that is close to where they live, work, or go to school. If for some reason on a particular evening, they are precluded from attending their home cell (e.g., an appointment of some kind), they can attend the small group of their choosing, knowing that they will have the same lesson on the agenda for sharing. The third benefit of the generic cell is that it is evangelistic in nature. Since the generic cell will be at multiple locations, it will facilitate the invitation by believers to their *oikos* network (family and friends) to attend a cell group.

We allot approximately one and one-half hours for our generic small group meeting, and we generally adhere to the format which we call the W-4, but we are flexible if there is a powerful move of God. The W-4 is an adaptation of the terminology from the traditional cell church language of the 4-Ws. The W-4 may be easier to remember and recall since most people fill out this tax form when they are hired for a new job or on an annual basis to change their tax status, number of exemptions, or additional dollars of withholding. Additionally, it provides the sequence of the cell meeting in numerical progressive order to make it easier to remember which segment comes first in the cell meeting. It also facilitates teaching when new converts or cell leaders are trained. This is not to say that a small group should not be flexible as the Spirit leads. The W-4 appears below.

W1 – Welcome – Arrival, greeting, light snack, introduction, and icebreaker (15 minutes)

W2 – Worship – Singing, playing musical instruments, CDs (15 minutes)

W3 – Word – Small group discussion about the biblical lesson (40 minutes)

W4 – Witness – Ministering to people through prayer, spiritual gifts, and strategic planning (20 minutes)

Figure 5.2. - W-4 schedule

The pastoral care or recovery small groups which we have currently in operation on a rotation basis are: DivorceCare; DivorceCare for Kids for ages five to twelve (DC4K); GriefShare; Single and Parenting; and Financial Peace. These five programs are Christian-based, meet for thirteen-week cycles for two hours each week, and are licensed only to churches. The recovery groups also have a maximum of ten people and serve two purposes. First and foremost, the purpose is to minister to people where they have a real need and walk beside them on their road to healing. Jesus always ministered to a physical need before He presented the Gospel. The second reason is that statistics show that 90 percent of people who attend these recovery groups come from outside the hosting church, with 50 percent of the attendees being either nonbelievers or unaffiliated with a local congregation.[118]

This is important to us, as we desire to concentrate on conversion growth and not transfer growth. We are witnessing that these groups can serve as "feeders" into the small groups, which then "feed" into the church. Recently, we started an accessibility ministry, that seeks to empower those who have special needs and challenges, but we realize we are the ones being ministered to through the gifts and talents they share. We have also initiated a Christian book club here in the Washington metro area that meets once a month in a local restaurant. This also follows our small group and transportation methodologies and has vision for multiplication.

Eventually, the vision will be to have: homogeneous cells (men, women, children, and youth); intergenerational cells (adults and children together); special interest cells (revolving around shared interest or hobbies); and specialized cells. These specialized cells will be targeted areas of ministry for which we have already done the research. These include military bases, college campuses, prisons, and hospitals. We even have plans to penetrate some of the 173 foreign embassies of world countries that are located in our city. We envision that we can reach our world without ever leaving the city because of the global diversity that is present. This makes it necessary for the creation of a missionary training track for this purpose.

CURRICULUM

For our generic community groups, we decided not to reinvent the wheel as it pertains to curriculum, since we are small and in our infancy. While our goal as a congregation is to utilize the Sunday sermon lessons in our small groups, for now we are using various small group Bible series and supplementing our own teaching plans. Most of our small group series last six to eight weeks by design, as it provides a reasonable commitment of time. This is very important, especially when attempting to reach the unchurched, as it might be difficult for people to commit to longer periods. The reality is that if they like what they are experiencing in this short six- to eight-week series, they will come back for the first session of the next series, which begins the next week after the conclusion of a series. For the maturing Christian, we offer a small group that is more focused on detailed teaching over a longer period of time that provides more substance.

The curriculum for the recovery small groups was purchased from Church Initiative. DivorceCare, GriefShare, and Single and Parenting have the same format: a three-segment program that consists of watching a 35-minute DVD from professionally trained Christian counselors, therapists, and pastors, entering into an hour discussion group based on the DVD, and weekly homework in the workbook that each member receives when registering. At the beginning of the class, the prior week's homework is discussed, and there is a five-minute break between the DVD and discussion. We close the session every week in prayer. The DC4K program is more fluid in its design and format, as it is structured for younger children. Financial Peace is a resource from Dave Ramsey, also licensed to churches to aid church members and the community in financial planning and reducing debt.

MULTIPLICATION

One of the goals implicit in the cell church and our small community groups is to multiply itself. Throughout cell church literature, it is commonly reported that the average time for multiplication is anywhere from six months to a year. I have selected a six-month target time frame for the multiplication of generic small groups at our church. The reason for this time period is not the quantitative growth opportunity, but rather it is qualitative. Here are some reasons that substantiate that claim.

A cell base of ten people is fewer than most groups that have twelve to fifteen people. At the same time, it is not too small to feel that there is a lack of group dynamics. It provides the opportunity for greater qualitative sharing, pastoral care, member participation, and the possibility for more rapid multiplication than having to obtain twelve to fifteen people in the group before multiplying. This keeps multiplication occurring in the DNA of the church.

Six months is one-half a year, which is twenty-six weeks. Since the cell group meets weekly, there would be twenty-six meetings to attend. By the second or third month, the group dynamics should solidify to the point that real community can be experienced.

The final three months should be very fruitful for the group. The danger of multiplying later than six months is that the group could turn "inward" to a maintenance mentality rather than focusing "outwardly" to multiplication and winning the harvest. Wolfgang Simson, author of *Houses That Changed the World: The Return of the House Churches*, notes this as an infectious disease. He writes, speaking of the house church, but his comments are also applicable to a cell church: "It is prevented from becoming a pious club, an isolated social gathering with '*koinonitis*'—a form of 'fellowship-infection' of an inward-looking and self-centered Christian group."[119]

Randy Frazee, author of the book *The Connecting Church: Beyond Small Groups to Authentic Community*, echoes these sentiments about the possible dangers of not multiplying a small group at the six-month interval. He states:

> The truth is, many small groups degenerate into social groups within six months, with just a token prayer offered at mealtime. Here's what I'm trying to say: You can have 100 percent participation in church-sponsored small groups, but it doesn't necessarily mean that the people in these groups are becoming more like Christ.[120]

Generally, people think "annually," and we have calendars, fiscal years, and numerical dates to remind us. With multiplication occurring annually, it may become another once-a-year, routine task, or it may seem far off.

Multiplication that takes place in six months provides encouragement, enthusiasm, and celebration, as each milestone has been reached. This fuels revival for the newly formed group and those that will follow as it sends a message that this can be accomplished in a reasonable time. If it takes too long for multiplication to occur, the "fire" may wane, and people might lose their enthusiasm.

Starting in January 2012, we moved to a weekly celebration service, and soon we anticipate that the small groups will use the outline of the message given in Sunday morning celebration for their sharing time. The positive aspect is that the small group members have an opportunity to reinforce what they heard on Sunday. They will be able to have personal study and reflection time from Sunday morning until their cell group meets in a few days and be ready to interact with the group sharing insights or asking questions.

Again, it is important to transmit the proper DNA to subsequent multiplied small groups and those that will lead those groups. If this means that it takes a little longer from time to time to experience multiplication, then so be it. The proper DNA transmission to daughter cells is imperative if the church is to thrive; otherwise, a genetic small group disease is being passed on, and it will mutate.

The recovery small groups will multiply but not in the traditional sense of cell multiplication, as it may take years for full healing of some of the members. However, as we see the need for these groups is huge, we will multiply the number of groups that exist. Perhaps some former members can participate in an administrative role for new groups, in addition to having the option to share their testimonies in ongoing meetings. In time, perhaps some will have healed and have the desire to lead their own groups. In this case, small group multiplication happens but perhaps at a slower, nonlinear rate. It is foreseen that once the homogeneous and intergenerational small groups are up and running, they could have the ability to mimic the generic cells in multiplication strategy. For more specialized small groups, college campus ministry, hospital, military, foreign embassy, and special interest, the multiplication strategy will exist but will have to be assessed based on individual circumstances.

THE EQUIPPING PROCESS

The equipping, or training, process is an integral part of our local assembly as it should be in yours. In the same fashion as humans are trained from young children to adulthood, Christians are to be trained from their conversion experience to become leaders in the local church. The biblical mandate is conveyed in Acts 4, where God gave the apostle, prophet, evangelist, pastor, and teacher the responsibility to equip the saints to maturity. While our community groups serve a great purpose in instruction, the Encounter is the foundational educational experience for new converts and those joining our assembly. The School of Leaders prepares and provides advanced training to members of our congregation in order to engage in leadership roles within the assembly.

NEW MEMBER ASSIMILATION: THE ENCOUNTER

The Encounter is a process by which new Christians are assimilated into the body of Christ and the local congregation soon after their conversion experience. It involves attending a weekend retreat, commencing Friday evening and concluding Sunday morning, away from the church campus. The purposes of the Encounter are: to assure believers of their newly found salvation; deal with the vices of sin; address hurts, wounds, and scars; and provide encouragement to live a victorious lifestyle. The ultimate goal is one of spiritual formation, discipleship, and transformation in the earliest stage of Christian development.

The Encounter is only the beginning for new converts. As the church enters into partnership with these new believers, we realize that standing beside them on their journey is a process. Further, one-on-one counseling, small group gatherings, a new member class, and additional seminars may be required. Our typical new-convert life cycle is depicted in figure 5.3.

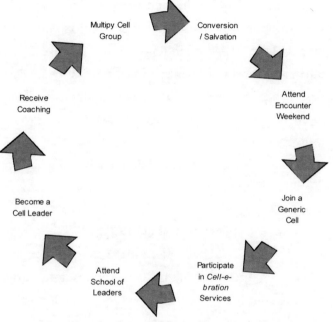

Figure 5.3 - New convert life cycle

While at the Encounter, we will address the new converts' needs through an agenda consisting of worship, prayer, instruction, small group sessions, recreation, meals, and community fellowship. We have identified Tides Inn in Irvington, Virginia, and Seven Oaks in Charlottesville, Virginia, as viable retreat centers that lend themselves to a holistic approach to ministry. These venues are away from the church campus and provide easy accessibility as they are within a two-hour driving distance from the Washington, DC, metropolitan region. They are also located close to water and the mountains, which sets the tone for tranquility away from the urban environment. These surroundings will assist new converts in getting in touch with themselves, each other, and, most importantly, God. Some of the amenities of these facilities include lodging, dining, breakout rooms for small groups, as well as a large meeting room for worship or joint sessions. Recreationally, they house golf, tennis, canoeing, fishing, biking, swimming, kayaking, yacht cruising, croquet, a sand beach, and a place to have a circle bonfire.

LEADERSHIP DEVELOPMENT: SCHOOL OF LEADERS

It has been discussed that the cell group is not to exist for itself, but it is to be fruitful and multiply in a short period of time. Where one cell existed, when multiplication takes place, it becomes two cells; two become four, and so on all over the Washington, DC, metropolitan region. As previously stated, we are ideally targeting a period of six months before multiplication occurs. Since multiplication is the goal of each small group, it is necessary that there be a constant pool of leaders available to lead new cell groups. The School of Leaders is where the "seeds of multiplication" reside.

The School of Leaders is a six-month, intensive training track, which we will encourage all new converts to attend after the Encounter weekend. This is based on the premise that everyone is capable, and God wants to use him or her in bringing in the harvest. The training is done through instruction and on-the-job training as an apprentice in an existing cell group. We are holding our School of Leaders training on Sunday morning prior to the Celebration Service.

Since new Christians will be on fire about their newfound faith and have close ties with their *oikos*, they may be able to win souls to Christ sooner rather than later by having this training early in their walk with God. When new converts complete the leadership training track, they participate in a graduation ceremony and are commissioned by the church to open up a new small group with the full backing and support of the Church. We are convinced that everyone can be used by God in this fashion; however, some may chose not to lead a group for whatever reason or circumstance. We have a policy of non-coercion, as it has to be a "free-will" decision.

This method is easily reproducible and instills the DNA of learning, evangelism, and multiplication in the new convert from birth. This behavior, when instilled at birth, is likely to be replicated throughout the life of the Christian. It also assists in planning purposes for future multiplication efforts, as it assures that there is a constant pool of leaders ready to take on newly multiplied cells. Your church would benefit by encouraging new converts or members to enroll in such a training track as soon as they become a part of your assembly. It will have long-term benefits that aid in pastoral care, member retention and evangelism.

CELEBRATION: THAT THEY ALL MAY BE ONE

Jesus uttered these words in prayer recorded in John 17:21: "That they all may be one." His prayer was for the unity of the apostles whom He would soon leave and for those who would be received into the church for all generations. Individual small groups are necessary for the church, but so is the celebration service. The celebration service makes it possible in a physical sense, so "that they all may be one." Both are necessary for the church to operate effectively and efficiently. In this section, I will describe the function and frequency of the celebration service, the numerical size, and the birthing of new celebration centers.

FUNCTION AND FREQUENCY

The function of the celebration service is to bring all the small groups together for corporate worship, edification, encouragement, and instruction. It is important for those who have come from more traditional church backgrounds to participate in a larger gathering. It also gives an opportunity for other cell leaders and members to mingle with each other to develop *koininia*. For the senior pastor, it is a time to speak to a united group and "share the vision" so that all can hear it under one roof. We are holding our weekly celebration services at a local school in the Washington, DC, metropolitan area, while our small groups meet weekly in other locations.

SIZE

Our assembly does not desire to become a mega-church. We desire to mimic the small-group "relational dynamic" in the celebration structure for the healthy corporate gatherings of small groups. This relational dynamic in celebration is often overlooked in cell church circles.

The illustration previously presented shows our small group model of a maximum of ten people in a small group, but it goes further to define that it takes a minimum of one hundred persons to constitute another celebration center. The one-hundred-person minimum is simply the maximum number of ten in a cell group multiplied by the same number. In other words, it represents the establishment of ten cell groups of ten people. We will call this process of establishing a celebration center 10^2 (ten squared). I hope to see the cell church move to a new mathematical paradigm that replaces the previous language of addition, division, and multiplication with one of exponential growth.

While the small group model is for illustrative purposes only, in reality the maximum number of people we would like to have in our celebration services is between 150 and 200. This maximum number of people connected to a particular celebration center recognizes the dynamics of relationships, and this is an effort to maintain those dynamics. In the book *The Tipping Point: How Little Things Can Make a Big Difference*, Malcolm Gladwell makes a case for and discusses the Rule of 150. He states, "The figure of 150 seems to represent the maximum number of individuals with whom we can have a genuinely social relationship, the kind of relationship that goes with knowing who they are and how they relate to us."[121]

Gladwell uses the illustration that with 20 people in a group, there are 190 two-way relationships to keep track of: 19 involving yourself, and 171 involving the rest of the group.[122] With 150 people in a group, this would further complicate things and compromise the group dynamics of sociability. It appears that the

Rule of 150 has great validity because this number has determined village size, the number of people fighting in military units, and the maximum number in a religious context. The religious group known as the Hutterites used the Rule of 150: when a colony approached 150 people, they split or multiplied it into two colonies.[123]

Howard A. Snyder and Daniel V. Runyon, authors of *Decoding the Church: Mapping the DNA of Christ's Body*, suggest that between one hundred and two hundred people should be the maximum number of attendees in a congregation. In relation to congregational size, they state:

> Given the sweep of Christian history, our hunch is that there is an optimal size, perhaps in the range of one hundred to two hundred people—more or less, depending on the context. Christian Schwarz's research suggests that on average, smaller churches grow more rapidly than larger ones and reports, "On nearly all relevant quality factors, larger churches compare disfavorably with smaller ones." Sociological studies show that as the size of a congregation increases, usually the commitment level decreases.[124]

While each church has to follow its unique vision, I concur with Gladwell, Snyder and Runyon that when the congregation grows to more than 150 to 250 people that the overall relational dynamics of the congregation begin to dilute. Also the opportunities for leadership and gift expression may diminish. In some infrequent and extraordinary cases, the possibility of a controlling mentality by leadership in a more subtle form may occur.

If your church is larger than the numbers expressed, I am not saying you are in error. After all, it was God that has blessed your church to get to the numerical size it is. Perhaps God desires for you to hold the course that you are on; if so, then please follow His instruction. However, He may be prompting you to move in new directions for the church health of members, leadership development, and extended mission, which in the long run will provide both quantitative and qualitative church health and growth. If God is guiding your heart in this direction, you may now be wondering what methodology can be implemented that will both maintain the larger vision intact and for things to operate smoothly. In the next two segments, I discuss the concepts of multiple celebration centers and a grand celebration that might provide some insight on the matter for your ministry environment.

BIRTHING NEW CELEBRATION CENTERS

One of the distinguishing characteristics of the cell church from a church with small groups is multiplication. There is multiplication of small groups, multiplication of cell leaders to facilitate the small groups, and multiplication of coaches. However, seldom does one hear about the multiplication of a celebration center with a new leader other than the senior pastor.

Some assemblies may schedule two or more services at the same location. If there are multiple venues, then the senior pastor preaches at each location on an alternate schedule, or those locations become video venues. A video venue is formed when the senior pastor is physically present at one location and speaks to other congregations in different locations via video. The senior pastor may even rotate congregations each week where the live message is presented.

In reality, it is practically impossible for one person designated "senior pastor" to adequately pastor multiple hundreds or thousands of people in one or more locations. Jesus gave a hint of this in the Parable of the Lost Sheep recorded in Luke 15, where a shepherd attended to one hundred sheep. Even if other associate pastors are on staff, the senior pastor cannot pastor all these people. Many in the congregation experience a disconnect with the senior pastor because he or she is not personally available to them when needed. The senior pastor becomes a motivator, coach, and administrator of other pastors.

The strategy that we have embraced at our assembly in Washington is to multiply celebration centers with new leaders. Once there is a minimum of one hundred people and up to a maximum of two hundred people, our desire is to start new celebration centers in the Washington metro area to maintain the equilibrium of relationship dynamics within a congregation. As small leaders multiply their cell groups of ten, they will be coaching these new leaders. Once the original small group leader of ten multiplies and establishes ten groups (10^2–ten squared) or more, a new celebration center will be established. The likely candidate to be the celebration-center pastoral leader is the person that multiplied ten groups.

We already have our first celebration center in Springfield, Virginia, and it is our plan at this time to establish a total of eleven celebration centers in the Washington metro region. The geographical locations of these additional ten celebration centers have already been identified and are planned in conjunction with the DOT Model that will be discussed in the next chapter. These celebration centers will not be a multisite-model video venue with me providing the Sunday sermon. Each celebration center will have its own regional leadership and be accountable to the WBCC network. My role will primarily shift from a pastor of one assembly to include coaching these celebration center leaders. This coaching will be done on a one-on-one and face-to-face basis at least monthly.

Once a month, all the celebration center pastoral leaders and their members will come together for a larger celebration gathering called "Grand Celebration."

GRAND CELEBRATION: GREAT CLOUD OF WITNESSES

When multiple small groups that meet weekly come together, it is called celebration. The multiplying of celebration centers has been discussed, but now the concept of multiplying the celebration experience itself will be expressed. As a regional church, WBCC envisions having multiple celebration centers comprised of small groups of ten at each location. Not only is it important for individual small groups to have a corporate worship experience, but it is necessary for the larger body of Christ (multiple celebration centers) to come together as well as a great cloud of witnesses. This is called Grand Celebration, and the function and frequency of this concept will now be discussed.

FUNCTION

The function of the Grand Celebration serves multiple purposes. One of these is to have a broader body of Christ corporate worship experience and fellowship. Additionally, this addresses the question of how cell members who were once together in other cell groups stay connected and maintain interaction.

One of the dilemmas was how to maintain a strategic balance of utilizing other qualified individuals in a pastoral role of leadership. Another was maintaining a relational atmosphere in our church (150 to 200 people per celebration center and not becoming a mega-church in the traditional sense) and the casting of vision from the senior pastor. This forum provides that platform.

A fear that may be prevalent for some pastors and congregations in having multiple celebration centers is that someone may gain too much influence and split the church. This, of course, carries other implications, such as human resources to get the job done and a budgetary impact. The concept of having Grand Celebrations for the celebration centers theoretically connects all the pastors and members of congregations to WBCC since they are located in the metro area (maximum one-hour drive) and provides a spillover-of-influence effect. While a split can still occur, it is more unlikely with such a gathering. As it is God's Church, and not mine, I as senior pastor am more concerned about the relational health of the church than the possibility of a split. With the proper checks and balances in place it is my conviction that a church split is less likely to happen. Could this be an option for your church in your city, especially if it has grown too big and the relationship factor seems to be lost?

FREQUENCY

The first Grand Celebration will be scheduled once there are two or more operational celebration centers. At the time of this writing, there is one celebration center located in Springfield, VA. The Grand Celebration will meet together once a month on a standard Sunday, perhaps in the afternoon or for an evening service.

The idea is for all celebration centers to come together as a corporate entity for worship, fellowship, encouragement, and vision casting from the senior pastor and leadership team to all the church members. This would be an ideal time to have communion service for the entire body. This could also serve as a time where celebration-center pastors and other outside speakers could address the entire church.

This chapter unveiled the basic tenets of the small-group network strategy for our church to foster community. You and the church that you lead will need to adopt a small group strategy for your congregation or denomination. This strategy then must be contextualized to your environment in order to be effective. I am convinced this can occur in many urban areas by utilizing the existing transportation infrastructure that will be discussed in the next chapter.

CHAPTER 6

TRANSPORTATION STRATEGY: DOT SMALL GROUP (CELL) MODEL^{SM}

In the Introduction, I proposed that the solution to traffic congestion experienced by those who attend church services can be found in decentralizing the church into small groups and in the modes of transportation that contribute to the dilemma. The small-group network strategy described in the previous chapter explains the basic concepts of decentralization into small groups, which reduces isolation, aloneness, and fragmentation, as well as creates community. However, it does not describe where and how these small groups might be deployed in Washington, DC, which would provide you a basic illustration to adapt these concepts for the church in your city.

It is obvious that each city is different in its geography and transportation infrastructure. In this chapter, I fill in the missing pieces by exploring our transportation-based network strategy, which is embedded in a new cell-model called, "DOT Small Group (Cell) Model^{SM}." While the presentation in this chapter and the next is illustrated for Washington, DC, chapter 8 provides some ideas on how to develop and contextualize this model for your city or region. The DOT Model serves as the "delivery system" for the small group network. In the Washington, DC ministry context, it has three modules: land, air, and water. The conceptualization of this model and the exploration of the three modules will be presented in this chapter.

CONCEPTUALIZATION OF THE DOT MODEL

The concept for the DOT Model resides in the geographical nature of the Washington Metropolitan Region and its transportation infrastructure. The goal of the model is the strategic placement of small groups in a city that is challenged by extreme traffic congestion and its fallout. The philosophy of the DOT Model can be summarized by the acronym MAPT. Phonetically, this is pronounced "mapped". Since our cell model is based on transportation, we desire the experience of our small group and church attendees to be all "mapt" out. MAPT takes into consideration the placement of small groups in locations that are mobile, accessible, proximate, and time-efficient (see figure 6.1).

Mobile – The location can be reached through convenient means of transportation

Accessible – The location is easy to get to

Proximate – The location is close to where people work, live, or attend school

Time efficient – Maximizes the individuals' time during congested commuting peak hours, enabling them to attend a small group wherever they are located, which will result in minimum frustration, providing a better quality of life spiritually, physically, and emotionally

Figure 6.1. - Explanation of MAPT.

There are three modules to the DOT Model: land, air, and water. Each module will be examined independently before integrating the entire model.

LAND MODULE

The land module is the largest component of the DOT Model and incorporates the modes of automobile and train transportation on the interstates and rail systems in this area. The centerpiece of the DOT Model is the Capital Beltway (I-495) in conjunction with the Washington Metrorail, known simply as "The Metro" in this community. The Capital Beltway (I-495) is a sixty-four-mile loop around the nation's capital and has sixty-seven exits. Each exit is about 1.7 miles from the next exit. Approximately 250,000 vehicles travel on the Beltway each day. It is interesting that the path of the Beltway takes it through the states of Maryland and Virginia and only briefly through the District of Columbia over the Potomac River on the Woodrow Wilson Bridge.

The Beltway is circular in nature and functions like the rim of a bicycle wheel. The "rim" (Beltway) is connected to "inner spokes," with roads and the train system connecting to the center of downtown Washington. The Beltway ("rim") also has "outer spokes" that connect to the suburban communities in Maryland and Virginia. These "outer spokes" are more symbolic of a "captain's wheel" on a sailing vessel. The main "outer spokes" highway arteries are: I-270 (northwest); I-66 (west); I-95 (northeast and southwest); I-395 (southeast); and I-595 (east). The "outer spokes" also extend as tentacles to communities in West Virginia and Pennsylvania.

The Metro is the primary transportation mode for the "inner spokes" operation of the DOT Model. Washington's Metro is the second largest rail-operated transportation system (behind New York City) in the United States. It is a combination of subway, surface, and aerial rail transportation that has five separate lines depicted by colors (blue, red, green, orange, and yellow), and these lines run in all directions from the center of Washington to the suburbs.

The Metro system covers 106.3 miles and has 86 rail stations throughout the Washington. DC, Metropolitan region serviced by 1,128 rail cars and 35 parking garages with 57,732 parking spaces. As of May 2010, the Metro had an average of 750,654 weekday passenger trips and, for fiscal year 2010, total passenger trips of 217,219,146.[125] The largest ridership day in the history of the Metrorail system with 1,120,000 riders was January 20, 2009, when President Obama was inaugurated.[126]

In comparison to mass rail transit systems in some other cities, the Metro is clean, safe, and accessible to the major points in and outside of Washington. These points of interest include tourist attractions, the business and federal government districts, foreign embassies, social meeting places, fifteen different universities, hospitals, medical centers, stadiums, arenas, the zoo, and shopping centers. The Metro also services the waterfront and Ronald Reagan National Airport, which is part of the air and water segment of the DOT Model to be discussed later in this chapter. The rail system operates Sundays through Thursdays from 5 a.m. until 12 a.m., and on Fridays and Saturdays from 7 a.m. to 3 a.m. During peak hours, trains run every six minutes (sometimes every one to two minutes) and every twelve to twenty minutes off peak.

Furthering the dynamic impact of the DOT Model is the Metrobus system. The bus system feeds into the rail system and provides additional options for the commuter who might not want to drive or does not own an automobile. We have a few small group locations that are jointly at major bus/train stations and a few others along major bus lines, with future plans to expand. As of May 2010, the daily bus-boarding count was 416,148, and for fiscal year 2010, total boardings were 122.7 million. On the bus line, there are 350 routes and 12,216 bus stops, with a fleet of 1,479 buses covering 1,500 square miles.[127]

There are three additional major rail lines that feed into the Washington, DC, area: Maryland Transit Authority Rail System (MARC), Virginia Railway Express (VRE), and Amtrak. Many of these three lines make stops at Washington Metro Stations, so local commuters have a choice when commuting in this Metropolitan area. There are also other municipal bus transit systems that feed into some of the local Metro Stations and have destinations out to some of our locations. These are: Alexandria Transit Company (Dash), Arlington Transit (ART), Fairfax Connector, Reston LINK, and the Potomac and Rappahannock Transportation Commission (OmniRide). What roads or public transportation options in your city come to mind? Please begin to think about this as you read the rest of this book.

AIR MODULE

The air segment of the DOT Model is primarily focused on Ronald Reagan Washington National Airport in Arlington, Virginia, although church leadership believes that, in the future, we can expand to Dulles and Baltimore-Washington International airports. The Blue and Yellow Lines of the Metrorail system stop at Reagan National Airport. This gives the phase "take the train to the plane" a whole new meaning, where we take the train to the airport for a small group meeting. The Metrorail orange line is currently being constructed to Dulles International Airport and is scheduled to be completed by 2016. Both National and Dulles have facilities where small groups can meet. I also serve as one of the volunteer chaplains at Reagan National Airport, so I am familiar with where these locations are.

As far as ministry opportunities, there are approximately fifteen-hundred people directly employed by both airports, along with employees of the TSA, USO, and concessionaires. If the airport is nearer than another venue, the general public has accessibility via the Metro. I recognize that some commuters might desire to meet at other locations but I have also learned never to limit the possibilities for God to work and make divine connections, even with people who might be traveling to other cities or countries.

WATER MODULE

The water module of the DOT Model looks to the Southeast Washington, DC, Waterfront on the Anacostia River where the Green Line of the Metro system stops. There are various places for the public to gather to enjoy time along the riverfront, including the Washington Nationals Ballpark. There are three other waterfronts on the Potomac River: Downtown Washington, DC; Old Town Alexandria, Virginia;

and National Harbor in Prince George's County, Maryland. All of these venues have shopping, entertainment, restaurants, and other activities and are accessible to public transportation.

The DOT Model takes the church to the people, instead of having people come to the church. It is truly marketplace ministry facilitated by transportation, which strategically targets small-group placement at these pivotal locations. As one reads and attempts to visualize such a massive transportation system, the possibilities for small-group strategic placement emerges, along with the multiplication of these groups. Now that the skeletal view of the DOT Model has been explained, the next section will apply flesh to the bones to see how it is relevant for us in Washington, DC and how it can be applicable for where you live and perform ministry.

THE DOT MODEL UNVEILED: THE INTEGRATION OF LAND, AIR, AND WATER MODULES

In Appendix A, the Washington Beltway Community Church DOT Small Group (Cell) Model is illustrated. This map was custom designed, is copyrighted, and is drawn to scale. There is a legend in the lower right-hand corner that provides basic information for the model. To facilitate understanding of the DOT Model, it is suggested that the reader refer to all of the relevant appendices indicated in this book.

The first module of the DOT Model is land, which is comprised of interstates (automobiles) and railways (trains). The Capital Beltway (I-495) circles the metro area as is depicted by the red, white, and blue interstate symbols. Interstates 66, 95, 270, 295, 370, 395, and 595 are identified by these interstate symbols. Major federal highways (US 1, US 29, and US 50) are identified by the white shield figure. The predominant state and county roads (4, 189, 267, 295, 355, and 390) are depicted by the white oval symbols. The District of Columbia is in the center of the Beltway and has a gold, diamond-shaped perimeter. The District in area is approximately ten square miles, neighboring Maryland and Virginia.

Paying particular attention to the perimeter of the Beltway (I-495), there are red houses with red-cross symbols. These identify targeted locations for small groups that are exit-based on the interstate system. The numeral inside the exit-based cells correlates to the DOT exit numbering system for easy identification in the DOT Map Key (See Appendix B). While additional exit-based locations for future groups are identified for interstates other than I-495, this serves the illustrative purpose without convoluting the map.

The Metrorail is identifiable on the map by the five broader lines, which are schematically colored in blue, orange, yellow, red, and green. Each of these colors actually corresponds to the name of the train and what "line" or route the train travels. These five lines service a total of eighty-six Metro Stations, forty in Washington, DC, twenty-six in Maryland, and twenty in Virginia.[128]

The Orange Line travels from New Carrollton, Maryland, to Vienna, Virginia, and carries 25 percent of Metrorail's daily ridership. The Blue Line's final destination points are Largo Town Center in Prince George's County, Maryland, and Springfield, Virginia. It accounts for 16 percent of total daily passengers. The Yellow Line starts at the Fort Totten section of Washington, DC, and ends at the Huntington Station in Alexandria, Virginia, having the fewest passengers at 8 percent. The Red Line boasts the largest daily ridership at 37 percent. Its origination point is in the Rockville, Maryland, area at Shady Grove Road, and it terminates in Glenmont, Maryland. The Green line connects Greenbelt and Branch Avenue, both in Prince George's County, Maryland, and comes in with 14 percent of total daily ridership.[129]

Looking at the map in Appendix A, each of the five Metro lines have small black crosses positioned along the Metro infrastructure. These crosses designate Metro Stations and the locations of future small groups. Stations that are located in Maryland and Virginia are identified by station names on the map, while those stations inside the District of Columbia have a numerical value assigned so the map would not be congested with information. The Metro-based cells inside the District of Colombia are linked to the Map Key in Appendix C in numerical, ascending station order.

The regional rail lines MARC and VRE are represented on the map (in Appendix A) by the thinner red (MARC) or blue (VRE) line with a small dot at each end of the line. The MARC Rail has three lines: Penn Line (Washington, DC—Union Station to Baltimore, Maryland—Penn Station), Camden Line (Washington's Union Station to Perryville, Maryland) and Brunswick Line (Union Station in DC to Martinsburg, West Virginia). The MARC Rail Penn Line route is significant since Baltimore's airport and train station have a direct line into Washington, DC. The VRE has two lines: Fredericksburg Line (Fredericksburg, Virginia, to Union Station in DC) and Manassas Line (Manassas, Virginia, to Union Station).

The black symbols positioned on the map that look like churches with a white "C" designated in the middle of the figure are the future locations of eleven celebration centers. All of these celebration centers are to be accessible by Metrorail or/and Interstate. The large purple church marker on the map is the strategic headquarters for Washington Beltway Community Church, which is in Springfield, Virginia, and is also home to one existing celebration center.

The air module (airport) is depicted on the map by the solid gray area, which currently is Ronald Reagan Washington National Airport. Again this airport is accessible by the interstate (I-66, 95, and 395) and Metrorail system (Appendix C #51). The water module (water-ports) can be viewed through the lens of both the interstate system (I-495, Appendix B #2A) and Metrorail (Appendix C #12, #13, and #25).

Now that the DOT Model has been explained, it is time to show how, on paper, it could impact chosen cell target areas. Table 6.1 shows the potential of this model for five target small groups. The table indicates in the first column the jurisdiction of the cell, whether in Washington, DC, Maryland, or Virginia. This column further communicates the approximate location in each jurisdiction as defined by rail stop or Capital Beltway exit location.

The second column depicts the mode of transportation (rail, automobile, bus, airport, or water). If multiple modes of transportation (train, auto, and bus) are accessible, these are listed, as well as if multiple rail lines (Metro, MARC, VRE, AMTRAK) stop at the same train station. The third column provides the particular rail line color for the Metro and link to the number stop on the WBCC DOT map key. There are numbers only for the Metro rail stations that are in the District of Columbia. The rest of the stations in Maryland and Virginia are identified by rail stop name.

The final column indicates the number of daily passengers frequenting these stops and/or intersections daily. The daily passengers for each of the five locations are designated as follows: Washington, DC, Union Station with 32,935 and Metro Center with 29,798[130]; Maryland at the Bethesda I-495/I-270 junction with 243,425 and the College Park I-495/I-95 interchange with 185,125[131]; and at the I-95/I-395/I-495 and Metrorail super junction in Springfield, Virginia, with 430,000 passengers[132]. As one can see, 920,993 people a day pass through these five areas. The number of daily passengers may, in fact, exceed 1,000,000 people a day because, where the number of car passengers is listed, that number really represents the number of automobiles, some of which may have more than one passenger.

Location	Mode of Transportation	Metro Line Color WBCC MAP Key #, or Beltway Exit No.	Number of Daily Passengers
Washington, DC – Union Station	Train – Metro, MARC, VRE, and AMTRAK	Red Line - #23	32,745
Washington, DC – Metro Center	Train – Metro	Red, Blue and Orange Line - #18	29,698
Bethesda, MD I-495/I-270 junction	Auto	I-495 Exit 35	243,425
College Park, MD I-495/I-95/ Junction	Auto	I-495 Exit25/27	185,125
Springfield, VA I495/I-95, I-395 Junction	Train – Metro, VRE Auto, Bus (Fairfax Conn/TAGS/Gryhd)	Blue Line I-495 Exits 57A-B, I-95 Exit 170B	430,000

Table 6.1 - WBCC DOT Small Group (Cell) Model^{SM} (5 small group target locations)

Additionally, where the mode of transportation is listed as either train or car, it can be both. This occurs at the junction, where the interstate meets the rail station (e.g., Springfield, Virginia, and College Park, Maryland). These statistics represent only one mode of transportation per location, so the total population is somewhat larger than the statistics illustrated in this table.

Since these locations are (MAPT) *mobile* (train, auto), *accessible* (easy to get to), and *proximate* (close to where people work, live, or attend school), they can attend cell groups and save *time* in commuting to these locations and home. Instead of sitting in a traffic jam and never making or being late for a midweek service, individuals can be productive with time and attend a small group meeting near them. Once the cell group has concluded in ninety minutes, then traffic is at a minimum. In some commutes, this may mean over an hour saved. If one takes a train to a cell group meeting, the person can access a train every six minutes, and this leaves the driving to someone else. Looking at the larger impact of the DOT Model, I would like to focus on the traffic volume of the Capital Beltway and Metrorail's top ten stations pertinent to daily ridership.

Table 6.2 below indicates the 2010 Annual Average Daily Traffic (AADT) on the Capital Beltway. The annual average daily traffic is the total estimated annual traffic divided by the number of days in the year. The traffic estimates are computed at or near each exit interchange. This would indicate how many vehicles travel over a certain intersection and not how many exit at each intersection. The statistics for the Maryland portion of the Capital Beltway (Exits 2 and 41) is provided by the Maryland State Highway Administration for 2010.[133] The traffic flow data for the Capital Beltway in Virginia (Exits 43-57B, 173-177B) is supplied by the Commonwealth's Department of Transportation for 2010.[134]

MD Exit Nos.	AADT	VA Exit Nos.	AADT
WW Bridge/VA-2A, 2B	191,981	43	226,000
3B	141,751	44	179,000
4A, 4B	147,581	45A, 45B	195,000
7A, 7B	147,581	46A, 46B	165,000
9	177,981	47A, 47B	175,000
11A, 11B	185,931	49A, 49B, 49C	180,000
13	n/a	50A, 50B	205,000
15A, 15B	203,000	51	178,000
16	204,481	52A, 52B	177,000
17A, 17B	213,841	54A, 54B	170,000
19A, 19B	231,801	57A, 57B/170B	349,000
20A, 20B	205,142	173	147,000
22	221,521	174	154,000
23	212,261	176A, 176B	135,000
24	216,421	177A, 177B	150,000
25	227,251		
27	243,471		
28A, 28B	213,207		
29A, 29B	215,841		
30A, 30B	232,941		
31	240,271		
33	239,001		
34	n/a		
35	116,211		
36	116,311		
38	266,381		
39	220,901		
40	n/a		
41	219,150		

Table 6.2 - 2010 Average Annual Daily Traffic Volumes (I-495)

While this information displays the traffic volume on the Beltway (I-495), which is the centerpiece of the interstate system for the DOT Model, the same information is available for all the interstates and major roads in the area. The Metrorail system's eighty-six stations have an average daily ridership of 750,654. While I have the statistics for the entire rail system, only the top ten busiest of these stations in terms of average daily ridership (totaling 238,128) appear below in table 6.3.[135]

MetroRail Station	Entries
Union Station	32,745
Metro Center	29,698
Gallery Place - Chinatown	25,894
Farragut North	24,105
Farragut West	23,137
Dupont Circle	22,907
L'Enfant Plaza	22,563
Foggy Bottom	21,587
Rosslyn	18,122
McPherson Square	17,370
	238,128

Table 6.3 - Ten busiest Metrorail stations – 2010
(average weekday ridership)

Washington Beltway Community Church has a physical presence in eight of these top ten busiest rail stations, along with some of the other eighty-six rail stations. This will be discussed in the implementation strategy presented in chapter 7. The statistics for the top ten Metrobus routes are available as well, but they will not be presented at this time. It is significant to say that our church has presence on two of the top ten bus routes with an average weekday ridership of 11,943 on Pennsylvania Avenue and 12,717 on 16th Street.[136]

The utilization of public transportation is thought by some to be relegated mostly to minorities, those that are stratified in a lower economic class, or do not own automobiles. If the DOT Model is to be success-ful for our church and for yours, it must be patronized by all sectors of society. The profile of the ridership of the Metrorail and Metrobus systems that appears below in table 6.4 tells an enormous story.[137]

Washington Metropolitan Area Transit Authority		Metrorail	Metrobus
Gender	Female:	53%	60%
	Male:	47%	40%
Education	Some college or less:	17%	44%
	College degree or more:	83%	56%
Employment	Employed:	80%	76%
	Not employed:	20%	24%
Household Vehicles	None:	2%	19%
	One:	25%	35%
	Two:	48%	30%
	Three+:	26%	16%
	Mean number of vehicles:	2.1	1.5
Age	18-35:	17%	30%
	36-55:	50%	42%
	56-75:	30%	23%
	Over 75:	3%	5%
	Mean number of years:	48.7	46.1
Race	White/Caucasian:	76%	45%
	Net: Minority:	24%	55%
	Hispanic/Latino:	3%	10%
	Black/African American:	17%	41%
	Asian/Pacific Islander:	4%	4%
Income	Less Than $75,000:	24%	54%
	$75,000 or more:	76%	46%
	Mean:	$93,710	$69,900
	Median:	$103,880	$68,110
Mean Number of Years Living in DC Area:		14.7	14.6

Table 6.4 - Metrorail/Metrobus Ridership Profile for 2008

As evident in the statistical information provided, the majority of those that utilize the Metrorail, 98 percent, have one or more vehicles, 53 percent are female, 83 percent have at least a four-year college degree or more, 80 percent are employed, of which 76 percent earn more than $75,000 per year, approximately 76 percent are Caucasian, and 83 percent of the total passengers are thirty-five years and over. The daily ridership on Metrobus is approximately 45 percent less than Metrorail's. However, the profile is equally astonishing, as 81 percent have one or more vehicles, 60 percent are female, 56 percent have a college degree or advanced education, 76 percent are employed, of which almost 46 percent earn $75,000 or more, 45 percent are Caucasian, and 70 percent of the total passengers are thirty-five years and over.

To simplify the illustration of the DOT Model, the other statistical ridership information for the other commuter rail systems (MARC, VRE) and the bus lines have not been presented. However, one can imagine how significantly this transportation-based network strategy could empower an already existing small-group model in an urban environment when implemented. Are initial ideas being formulated in your mind as you think about the possible implications of such a strategy for your city or region of the world? In the next chapter, the process is discussed where the small group and transportation-based models are merged together for real-life implementation for the church.

CHAPTER 7

IMPLEMENTATION:
THE TWO SHALL BECOME ONE

The small group and transportation network strategies were discussed independently in chapters 5 and 6, respectively. The reasoning is that the small group philosophy and model for your church might look different from what I have presented in this book. It is critical that your small-group church strategy be in place before adapting a transportation-based model. Also, every region in the world will have a slightly different design to their transportation infrastructure than that which is presented in chapter 6. However, the small group strategy is interdependent with the transportation model for successful application.

This chapter describes merging the two strategies for effective implementation in our ministry context here in Washington, DC. The goal of the illustration in this chapter is to provide the readers with ideas that might spark creative ideas for your church and denomination as you begin to reflect how you could merge small groups with transportation for maximum effectiveness in your city. The DOT Model's four-phased implementation rationale will be discussed, which has been tailored for our congregation in the Metropolitan region. Remember, you will have to tailor it for your region as well. The four phases of the DOT Model are presented in areas of focus and prioritization, but they are not always linear in actual implementation. In chapter 8, I will provide some helpful areas in which to start brainstorming about the possibilities for implementing the DOT Model in your city.

Phase I pinpoints implementation inside the circumference of the Capital Beltway, while Phase II concentrates outside the perimeter of the Beltway. Phases I and II represent the land module that utilizes the automobile/interstates and trains/rail lines. Phase III examines the air (airport) and water (waterfronts) modules, with Phase IV taking a look into future expansion of the DOT Model, including a full bus design.

IMPLEMENTATION RATIONALE: THE TWAIN SHALL ALWAYS MEET

The idiom, "Never the twain shall meet," implies that two things which are so different do not have the opportunity to unite. This was most likely used the first time by Rudyard Kipling in his 1892 barrack-room ballad, "East is east and west is west and never the twain shall meet," depicting the gulf of understanding between the British and the inhabitants of the Indian subcontinent.[138] Small group models and transportation models function independently of one another and are not thought of as bedfellows. On the surface, merging the two may be inconceivable to many. However, I take the approach that "the twain shall always meet" and that the "two shall become one."

The DOT Model focuses on the strategic geographic placement of small groups along the existing transportation infrastructure where the small group structure can be layered on top of the geographic model. When the two become one, it is powerful in application for daily use and the multiplication of small groups. The rationale is to find the locations where people can travel (mobile) easily (accessible), that are close (proximate) to where people are, that people can reach quickly (time-efficient), and then use the small group model in those locations.

Our church has secured multiple locations in the double digits along the transportation infrastructure that are within one to two blocks of Metrorail stations or near the interstate system, where we can have small group meetings. These facilities are state of the art for any meeting, with full audio-visual capabilities. Currently, we have the facilities to host 140 small group meetings a week, outside of the main place of worship, if we had sufficient human resources. We now have multiple small groups meeting in a number of these locations around the Washington, DC, metro region. When multiplication occurs, we do not have to find other facilities, as we can use the same small group facility or any of the alternatives on a different day. We have identified additional prime locations that are suitable for the DOT Model as we grow numerically and geographically.

PHASE I:
INSIDE THE CAPITAL BELTWAY

The first phase of implementing the merged models is within the circumference of the Capital Beltway. Our strategy, although not always linear, is first to place small groups in locations that are within the Beltway because this is where the majority of people live, work, and go to school. However, the spontaneous expansion of the church may require starting small groups outside the Beltway during this time.

The epicenter of the Beltway and Washington, DC proper is the United States Capitol Building (E. Capitol St. E. and 1st St. NE, Washington, DC 20001). One of several demographic profile analyses that we have is based on four radii-strata (ten, twenty, forty, and sixty miles) from the U.S. Capitol epicenter. One way to look at this is to view the US Capitol as the center of a target, with several layers of rings that circles the bulls-eye. The implementation plan seeks to phase the placement of small groups along the transportation system, first within ten miles of the Capitol, then twenty, forty and sixty. The city of Washington, DC, is ten square miles, and the farthest extent of the Beltway from the US Capitol is no more than twenty miles, which is Phase I of our plan. All of the three modules of the DOT Model (land, air, and water) can be located within the Beltway's borders.

The first item in implementation was to choose the primary area for the headquarters and nerve center for our operations. Springfield, Virginia, was chosen because it is a prime location for the DOT Model. Looking at the WBCC Model Map, it is situated on the perimeter of the Beltway at the juncture where I-95, I-395, and I-495 meet (Exits 57A-B/170 B), and

430,000 people pass through that intersection daily on the interstates. This location is one of the places where the massive interstate system meets the rail system.

Springfield is the origination station for the Blue Line of the Metrorail system, which 9,665 people ride daily.[139] This location has far-reaching tentacles to the Virginia suburbs as people drive to Springfield to park their cars and take the train. Also, the Virginia Railway Express and Greyhound Bus Station have hubs at the Springfield Metro Station. Also, many regional bus services feed into the rail system here. With the additional ridership, it is easy to say that 450,000 people pass through this area each workday. Our first small-group weekly gathering started in Springfield, and this is where our first Celebration Center is located where our small groups gather together for Sunday worship.

Our assembly has meticulously identified and secured fifteen other small group locations, seven in Washington, DC, two in Maryland, and six in Virginia. One of the Washington, DC, locations is located across the street from the United States Capitol Building and two blocks from the Supreme Court and Union Station (#23—WBCC DOT MAP), which has 32 million people pass through its doors every year and has an average of over 87,671 people a day.[140] Union Station is the hub of Washington's transportation network, with Washington Metrorail, AMTRAK, MARC, and Virginia Railway Express (VRE) providing train services. Also bus service is represented by Washington Metrobus, Maryland Transit Authority, Loudoun County, Virginia Commuter Bus, DC Circulator, and PRTC Buses. It also serves as the tourist industries center for regional and local tours. Union Station is also host to many restaurants, bookstores, clothing, and variety stores and is frequented by travelers, commuters, residents, and area workers. There is also ample parking at Union Station for bicycles and for 2,448 vehicles.[141]

Union Station ranked first in Metro daily ridership with 32,745 commuters.[142] This number does not include commuters who take VRE, MARC, and other forms of transportation into the Maryland, Virginia, and West Virginia suburbs that might be candidates to attend our small groups. Another small group conveniently meets just steps from the Dupont Circle Metro Station (#6—WBCC DOT MAP), which is ranked sixth with 22,907 daily riders, serving the Red Line.[143] Four of the remaining five of the Washington, DC, locations are all within two blocks of the White House, and two of them have a prestigious Pennsylvania Avenue address. All four venues are one to two blocks of the following Metro Stations:

Metro Center (#18—WBCC DOT MAP), ranked second busiest with 29,698 daily commuters, which is the center of the Metro System servicing the Blue, Orange, and Red Lines; Farragut North (#5—WBCC DOT MAP) ranked fourth busiest with 24,105 commuters, servicing the Red Line; Farragut West (#4—WBCC DOT MAP) ranked fifth busiest with 23,137 daily riders, servicing the Blue and Orange Lines; and McPherson Square (#17—WBCC DOT MAP) ranked tenth busiest with 17,370 riders, servicing the Orange and Blue Lines.[144] The last Washington, DC venue is in the prestigious section of Georgetown, within walking distance from the Orange and Blue Line's Foggy Bottom/George Washington University Metro Station (#3—WBCC DOT MAP) ranked eight busiest with 21,587 passengers.[145] These seven stations alone handle 171,549 Metrorail riders daily, not to mention those who take other forms of transportation. It is realistic to say that our church has potential access to over 250,000 people on a daily basis just in the city limits of Washington, DC. This is due to meeting in the marketplace in the center of the federal district where thousands work, live, and commute from locations that are convenient to the transportation infrastructure. Can you imagine how this strategy would impact your city with the Gospel?

Our two Maryland locations are in Chevy Chase and Bethesda, Maryland. Chevy Chase is actually on the District/Maryland line, and our small group venue in Chevy Chase is directly across the street from the Friendship Heights Metro Station (#2— WBCC DOT MAP) servicing the Red Line with 9,804 daily passengers.[146] This station also services the Montgomery County Maryland Ride-On Bus system and the Washington Metro Bus System, whose numerical ridership is not reflected above. This location also has an upscale shopping mall across the street with a movie theater complex and multiple venues for dining. It is near Exit 33 of the Capital Beltway (I-495). For this and all the daily passenger statistics for the Capital Beltway (I-495) exits, please see table 6.2. Our Bethesda location is one block from the Bethesda Metro Station (labeled "Bethesda" on WBCC DOT Map) servicing the Red Line with 10,605 daily passengers.[147] This is also a hub for the Washington Metro Bus system and is situated not far off Exit 34 of the Capital Beltway (I-495) and near the trendy Bethesda Row, where scores of restaurants and a movie theater are located.

Our six Virginia locations are at King Street, Alexandria, Old Town Alexandria, Rosslyn, Reston, and two in Tyson's Corner. The King Street location is directly across the street from the King Street Metro Station, which services the Blue and Yellow Lines, with a daily ridership of 8,991.[148] This location is near I-395, off Exit 5, which bears its name, and close to Exit 176 off the Capital Beltway (I-495). The Old Town Alexandria location is part of the DOT water module, as it is three blocks from the Potomac River Waterfront and art galleries, boutiques, shopping, and restaurants. This location is serviced by the Capital Beltway (I-495) and is located off Exit 177B. The nearest Metro Station is Braddock Road (seven blocks away) servicing 4,524 people daily on the Blue and Yellow Lines. Both of these Alexandria locations are serviced by DASH, which is the Alexandria Bus System and feeds into both Metrorail stations.

The Rosslyn (#41—WBCC DOT MAP) location overlooks the Potomac River in Arlington, Virginia. It is approximately three blocks from the Metro servicing the Blue and Orange Lines, ranked ninth with a daily ridership of 18,122 and has an exit off I-66.[149] There is a free shuttle in case one did not want to walk. This location is directly across the Key Bridge and is in walking distance to the historic section of Georgetown in Washington, DC, home of Georgetown University.

The two Tyson's Corner locations and the Reston venue are prime locations for the DOT Model, because these venues are right across the street from two of the largest shopping malls in the Washington Metropolitan Region. Tyson's Corner is home of the Tyson's Corner Mall and is at Exit 47 off the Capital Beltway (I-495) and has a shuttle. Tyson's Corner is the future site of a Metro Station on the Orange Line, scheduled to be open by 2013, which will only increase volume to this location. Reston's claim to fame is the Reston Town Center, and there is a local shuttle called the "Link" which transports passengers between the Town Center and the West Falls Church Metro Station (labeled West Falls Church on the WBCC DOT MAP), servicing the Orange Line with 10,836 passenger daily.[150] The Reston location is only six miles from Dulles International Airport, to which the Orange Line will extend in 2016.

What is more specific about the Metro System is that it is built around various points of interest and where people work, live, and attend school. This includes tourist attractions, college campuses, military bases, and foreign embassies. These locations are part of our ministry focus.

Every small group member has access to real-time information about the Metro System to plan his or her trip to a small group location by logging on to the Metro website or calling Metrorail information. Information is also available on any delays or problems on the system, and small group members can receive text information updates. For those driving, Trafficland.com provides real-time information concerning any traffic delays as well as traffic reports on the radio and television every ten minutes. With MapQuest, Google, Global Positioning Systems, and cell phones with Internet access, the small group attendee has every possible advantage in the twenty-first century with the DOT Small Group (Cell) Model. These examples of the DOT Model implementation are locations that our church presently has in place and represent a sample of the merger of the small group and transportation models for Phase I. It would be impossible in the scope of this book to articulate the positioning of small groups for every location, but it is representative of the reach and potential for ministry. Can you begin to conceptualize how such a strategy might be possible in the ministry of your church in the area of the world where you live?

The Celebration Center locations for Washington Beltway Community Church have been logistically identified to correlate with the small group structure. The goal is to eventually have eleven Celebration Centers strategically located at both ends of the Blue, Orange, Red, and Green Metro Lines, with the Yellow Line having only one Celebration Center in Huntington. Three are located in Virginia, six in Maryland, and two in Washington, DC.

The Virginia locations are Franconia-Springfield (Blue Line), Huntington (Yellow Line), and Vienna/ Fairfax George Mason University (Orange Line). Maryland is represented by Shady Grove in Rockville (Red Line), and Glenmont (Red Line), Greenbelt (Green Line), New Carrolton (Orange Line), Largo Town Center (Blue Line), and Branch Avenue (Green Line). The two Celebration Centers that will reside in the District of Colombia proper are at Metro Center and L'Enfant Plaza. The rationale for choosing these sites for Celebration Centers rests in the geographical nature of the Metropolitan Washington, DC, area and the transportation infrastructure.

The City of Washington, DC, is approximately ten square miles, with the US Capitol building located at the intersections of East Capitol Street, NE, and 1st Street, NE, being the accepted epicenter. The Capitol Beltway is no more than twenty miles in any given direction from the US Capitol. Six of the nine Metrorail and proposed Celebration sites are located at the end of Metro lines, which begin or end in Maryland or Virginia, where they intersect with the Capital Beltway. This translates to a location where rail and auto transportation can access the same location and maximize the potential for a strong, vibrant coming-together of individuals from the various cell groups. This would include those that live inside the Beltway, at the Beltway, or outside of the Beltway. In many cases, commuters who live twenty to forty miles outside of the Beltway will drive to this location as there is ample parking, and it is routine for them. This approach takes a "reaching out" as well as a "reaching in" position.

The two Celebration Centers (Metro Center and L'Enfant Plaza) in Washington, DC, were chosen for accessibility and volume of passengers. The Metro Center Station is the hub of all activity for the Metrorail system, and three out of the five rail lines (Red, Blue, and Orange) come into this station. The Metro Center Station also is the second busiest Metrorail station with 29,698 daily riders. L'Enfant Plaza is the only Metro Station that has four of the five lines (Yellow, Green, Orange, and Blue) meeting in a single location. L'Enfant Plaza is the seventh busiest station, having 22,563 daily riders.[151] The Virginia Railway Express, which has two lines—Manassas, Virginia, to Washington, DC (West-East), and Fredericksburg, Virginia, to Washington, DC (North-South)—also stops at L'Enfant Plaza.

The Grand Celebration that will bring together all the celebration centers will meet at Springfield, as this is the headquarters. It also has the best potential for traffic and rail access and WBCC's current facility can accommodate up to fifteen hundred people. It is our goal to populate Phase I locations inside the Beltway within five years, and we are off to an energetic start. Phase II looks toward those locations outside of the Capital Beltway, to which this book now shifts.

PHASE II:
OUTSIDE THE CAPITAL BELTWAY

Phase II of implementation concentrates outside the perimeter of the Capital Beltway using the DOT land module. A segment of this phase would entail placing small groups near only a handful of Metrorail stations, as most are within the circumference of the Beltway. Out of eighty-six stations, seventy-three are nestled inside the Beltway, while the remaining thirteen are not. A total of eight stations (Shady Grove, Rockville, Twinbrook, White Flint, Grosvenor-Strathmore, Forest Glen, Wheaton, and Glenmont) are on the Red Line in Montgomery County, Maryland; two stations (Dunn Loring-Merrifield) are on the Orange Line in Fairfax County, Virginia; one station (Huntington) is on the Yellow Line in Fairfax County, Virginia; and two are on the Blue Line—one

(Franconia-Springfield) in Fairfax County, Virginia, and one (Largo Town Center) in Prince George's County, Maryland. The Springfield and Dunn Loring stations are barely over the Beltway (I-495), as I-495 Exits 57A-B/170B and 49A-C have signage for these stations respectively. Again, phasing is not always linear, as we have a small group meeting at Springfield. Also the Virginia Railway Express (VRE) and the Maryland Transit Authority (MARC) have rail service outside the Beltway with stations at key locations near the Interstate System.

The Interstate mode of the land module is focused on I-95, I-66, and I-270. I-370 and I-595 are secondary targets. Interstate 95 is the major north-south vein on the east coast, and, in going north, the focus would be from the Beltway at College Park, Maryland, to Columbia, Maryland, and looking southward from Springfield, Virginia, to Fredericksburg, Virginia. The identified area on I-66 is from Vienna, Virginia, to Front Royal, Virginia. Finally, I-270 would determine areas for small group placement between Rockville and Frederick, Maryland. Along these routes are college campuses such as Mary Washington University, Johns Hopkins University, and multiple branches of Strayer University, along with military bases such as Fort Belvoir and Quantico Marine Base, to name a few prominent areas for ministry. The addition of new small groups to the WBCC network would require the addition of celebration centers outside the Capital Beltway to maintain the relational dynamics that we strongly embrace.

PHASE III:
AIRPORTS AND WATERFRONTS

The third phase of implementation is utilizing the air and water modules of the DOT Model. The air module features Ronald Reagan Washington National Airport, and the water module identifies locations along the Potomac and Anacostia waterfronts. The air module was the last segment of the DOT Model conceptualized and thought to be the most difficult and last implemented, but it was actually easier than I imagined.

The air module began in 2010, at at Ronald Reagan National Airport. This is where we held our GriefShare 13 week recovery small group. The airport is accessible on the Blue and Yellow Lines of the Metro System (#51—WBCC DOT MAP) and has 6,414 daily riders.[152] National Airport is also conveniently located off I-395 and the George Washington Parkway and near I-66, I-95, and I-495. The real possibility exists in the future to expand to Dulles International Airport, as the two airports are operated under the same umbrella. This will be of significant importance as the Metrorail project to Dulles Airport should be completed in 2016.

The water module is the final module of the DOT Model, the placement of small groups proximate to places where people congregate near the area's rivers. We have secured one location in Old Town Alexandria that is three blocks from the Potomac Waterfront and near the I-495 (Capital Beltway) interchange at Exit 177B. Another location in the planning stage is one exit away on the Beltway at National Harbor (Exit 2A), which is the first exit in Maryland after crossing over the Woodrow Wilson Bridge. Metrorail stops for the Navy Yard (#13—WBCC DOT MAP) and Anacostia (#25—WBCC DOT MAP) are also prime candidates for expansion of the water module.

PHASE IV: FUTURE EXPANSION

One of the anticipated areas of future expansion of the DOT Model is to strategically create a logistical grid for bus transportation, most of which feeds into the Metrorail System. The largest of these bus systems is the MetroBus, operated by Washington Metro Area Transit Authority (WMATA), who also operate the Metrorail system. Metrobus has routes in Washington, DC, Maryland, and Virginia, and services the rail stations. The ridership statistics for Metrobus have already been presented, and the information is readily available to create such a grid. The regional transportation bus lines in the area will need to be plotted and mapped to DOT Model specifications. These lines include the Alexandria Transit Company (DASH), Arlington Transit (ART), Fairfax Connector, Loudoun County Commuter Bus Service, Potomac and Rappahannock Transportation Commission (OmniRide), Reston LINK, Ride On (Montgomery County, Maryland), Tysons Transportation Association, Inc., and the Transportation Association of Greater Springfield (TAGS).

A visionary of the church must continually look into the future, as city planners do. To accomplish this feat, the church that implements the DOT Model in their region must be prayerful, project the anticipated culture, and be on the cutting edge of innovative thinking. This translates into continuing education for pastors, denominational executives, and the personnel in your churches that will be tasked with the operation of the DOT Model.

Another key to discerning the future is having people on your staff who represent every age, economic and educational level, and ethnic strata. Listening to these individuals will prove to be invaluable. It is also important to listen to others' voices in the community.

A key factor for churches and denominations that implement the DOT Model around the world is to listen to regional transportation planners. This can easily be accomplished by watching and listening to news reports through various forms of media. What might be extremely helpful is to visit the website of the jurisdictions in your region that are responsible for transportation to see what new projects might be underway soon, as well as anticipated completion dates for these projects. This way you can prepare the groundwork to expand the DOT Model in your city.

For instance in the Washington, DC, region there is a future Metrorail expansion scheduled, which would include the introduction of the Silver and Purple lines, as well as the expansion of the Orange, Blue, and Green lines.[153] The new Silver Line and Orange Line expansion would connect service to Dulles International Airport and points west. This would include communities such as Reston, Herndon, Tysons Corner, Manassas, and Leesburg, Virginia. This is scheduled to be completed in 2016, barring the consequences of politics.[154] There is a proposal to build a Purple Line, linking Bethesda and Silver Spring, Maryland, thereby connecting the two branches of the Red to the north of Washington by rail. Later, it would possibly be extended to New Carrollton, Maryland, thus connecting branches of the Green and Orange lines and eventually around the entire Capital Beltway, linking all the Metro endpoints together.[155]

The Blue Line is under consideration for expansion from Springfield, to Ft. Belvoir, Virginia. With the ongoing Base Realignment and Closure (BRAC), 18,000 jobs are expected to move to Ft. Belvoir by 2012; therefore, new interest has been placed on this possible extension.[156] Maryland has proposed extending the Green Line from the current northern terminus in Greenbelt to connect with Baltimore-Washington International Airport via Fort Meade, home of the National Security Agency. The link would be built in the next two decades to accommodate some of the growth expected in the Howard and Anne Arundel County regions as jobs move in with the recent military reorganization.[157]

Other innovative transportation ideas in the Washington metro region have emerged, including streetcar-light rail lines. One has been proposed at Columbia Pike in Arlington, VA, which would connect Fairfax and Arlington counties in Virginia and the Pentagon City Metro Station. In the District of Columbia, ground has been broken on a light rail line in the Anacostia area, which will connect passengers to the Metrorail system and go to Bolling Air

Force Base. One project underway is the Corridor Cities Transitway (CCT), which will link Clarksburg, Maryland, in northern Montgomery County with the Shady Grove station on the Red Line. There are also ongoing discussions for a light rail system for the Southern Maryland counties of Charles and St. Mary's. This line would grow from the Southern terminus of the Green Line (Branch Avenue) and connect to the rapidly growing area of Waldorf and other towns along MD Route 5.[158] The Inter-County Connector (ICC) is one project that we kept our focus on that is now complete. The ICC is indigenous to Montgomery and Prince George's Counties in Maryland, creating a road that links I-95 in Prince George's County to I-270 in Montgomery County.

This look into the future by your church and denomination is not about new roads and rail lines; it is about people—people that have a soul. When and where new infrastructure is designed, people will be found working, learning, and living there. These same people need love, fellowship, and a chance to experience God. It is because of people that your church should be there when these expansions take place and use the DOT Model to reach them with the good news of Jesus Christ, by strategically placing small groups near these locations.

Looking into the future should be broader than your own ministry setting. The future should include preparing others in your congregations and denominations that have a calling to start churches in other locations, both domestic and foreign. The question now is how might you begin to develop such a model for your congregation, denomination, and those that you will train, and what are the possible steps in the process? In the next chapter, I address this very question to assist in tailoring the DOT Model to your specific context in the world.

CHAPTER 8

DESIGN YOUR TRANSPORTATION-BASED SMALL GROUP MODEL

This chapter will offer some suggestive preliminary ideas of how you might develop a strategy for your church or denomination on how to formulate a transportation-based small group network in your region. I also discuss the importance of sharing the information and training others in your religious circles, once you have successfully implemented. Finally, I discuss the necessity for continuous evaluation of the effectiveness and efficiency of the DOT Model for your church, to identify what is working well and what, if any, corrective actions steps should be taken. This process is of extreme importance in having a vibrant, relational, and healthy transportation-based network of small groups in your city.

Please let me reemphasize that this book is not a how-to manual. There are too many unknown variables to investigate in each setting on a national or global scale. However, it can serve as a guide to spark creative ideas for you to seek the guidance of the Holy Spirit for your church's mission in the metropolitan region that it serves.

WHERE TO BEGIN IN DESIGNING THE DOT MODEL FOR YOUR CITY

In previous chapters of this book, I discussed some of the prerequisite steps before you begin the process of designing the DOT Model that can be adaptable for your region. These items included: knowing the dynamics of your congregation, knowing your wider community, developing a theology of small groups and transportation that can be substantiated biblically, and selecting a small group model. All of these steps should be well documented, with everyone buying into the process. This includes pastor, boards, church members, and denominational officials.

As you begin to think about these prerequisites, you will have to consider the human resources or personnel available to you. Will you personally do the necessary research and documentation, will a volunteer committee perform these services, or do you explore the option of hiring a consultant that will work with church personnel? The method chosen, of course, might depend on the available time, training, and expertise, financial considerations, and how soon you would like to move forward in implementing such a strategy. However you proceed, this will likely involve months of work and meetings, so you will have to be committed to the process.

Once these preliminary steps have been tackled, you are ready to begin work on the strategy of your DOT small-group delivery system. This too will take months to develop, document, and implement. So again, human resources, financial considerations, and the timing when you want to merge your small group system with the transportation-based DOT Model for implementation will be factors in the decisions that will have to be made.

The DOT Model strategy is unique to each context. This will be the most difficult part of the process. Therefore, it is impossible for me to speak in specifics at this point for your region, but I can suggest some general ideas for your consideration based on years of work in developing the model.

The DOT Model is designed with the urban city or region in mind and would be most effective in cities with a population of one million or more. The premise is that if there is a larger population, there should be a transportation infrastructure already in place. This might include interstates, some sort of rail or trolley system, and perhaps a bus system. Although the DOT Model might be most effective in large cities, this is not to rule out the possibilities of the DOT Model being implemented in smaller cities or even rural communities.

In the 1950s, the Eisenhower Interstate system in the United States was conceptualized and implemented over a number of years. Many of the highways developed then are main arteries in smaller cities and rural communities. Today, new interstates are being opened to make life and living more accessible and time-efficient for millions who previously were denied access. If you live outside the USA, you most likely have transportation infrastructure that is in place or soon will be. I want to inform you that a rail system, airport, or waterway is not necessarily required to be successful in implementing the DOT Model. What is necessary is the God-given calling to a particular ministry environment and the vision to see "the unseen" that lies in all communities.

The first bit of information to be shared with the pastor, church, or denomination in implementing the

DOT Model is that one of the keys to "seeing the unseen" is to accept your ministry assignment. This is true regardless of where God physically has your church located, knowing that God will provide information, inspiration, and creativity, in addition to supplying all your needs to accomplish the task. In general terms, God does not usually give us all the facts upfront for a multitude of reasons, but we must trust Him and go; and then the plan gradually unfolds.

To see the unseen implies that those who desire to implement the DOT Model must "exegete" their city. Exegesis is a principle practiced in theology, where one "brings out" the meaning of the biblical text in order to make it relevant to the readers or hearers. To bring out, one must look and study the text sometimes repetitively. To exegete a city, the pastor, church, or denomination who wishes to implement the DOT Model must look and study their city and region.

Ray Bakke and Jon Sharpe, authors of *Street Signs: A New Direction in Urban Ministry*, write that cities have history and personality.

> Puritan Boston had a public theology and Boston was to be a classic "city on the hill," it was to model a theological worldview, not only in its sanctuaries on Sunday but in its cultural, economic, and political structures as well.... Meanwhile Philadelphia was founded by the

Friends, or Quakers, and Quaker theology is intensely personal. It works from inside out, rather than outside in, or maybe in Boston's tradition, from the top down. Philadelphia became the classic home city for insurance companies or we might call it the capital of privatized faith in the "citizen save thyself" American tradition.

Other grids may also shape our understanding. For example, Washington, DC, New Delhi, and Brasilia function as capital cities. New York and Los Angeles in the United States and Mumbai and Bangalore in India clearly function as commercial cities. They drive national and increasingly global agendas, but do so differently than political capitals. People live and work in these various cities in vastly differing ways. On the other hand, we might describe San Francisco, Paris, and Rio as cultural cities, whose exports, near and far, are ideas, fashions, and trends. Other cities have industrial personalities.[159]

Those that desire to implement the DOT Model must read as much history as possible about the city where they are implementing. Encyclopedias and the Internet are useful tools, but extremely helpful are travel guides, such as *Insight Guides*, which give the prospective church that implements the DOT Model a history of the area as well as the current climate of the city in every aspect. Most pertinent for the DOT Model is the "how-to-get-around" section.

In exegeting the city, the prospective implementers of the DOT Model should understand that there are cities within the city. Bakke and Sharpe weigh in on this important point.

> There is no one city; but there are many sectors to a city. Here are some to think about: a commercial city, media city, ethnic city, political city, convention city, institutionalized city, theater and art city, athletic city, restaurant city, health and human services city, airport city, university city, commuter city and so on. Huge, diverse populations live in these sectors.[160]

In each sector of these cities within cities, people have to travel in and out of these areas. Some utilize multiple modes of transportation because of where they are located, and others rely exclusively on one or two forms of transportation. Those that desire to implement the DOT Model should purchase maps of the ministry setting and meticulously study these maps. Another suggestion is to investigate online information about the local commuter transportation systems. You should be able to obtain information from your state's highway administration, which would provide statistical information and possible future projects in the planning stages. If you live outside of the USA, contacting the equivalent agency may be of some help.

You might desire to utilize a consultant to assist you in this quest, as it is time-consuming. If you do, the consultant should express to those that engage him or her that the pastor, church, or denomination must have a vested interest in implementing the DOT Model in their city. This vested interest should include some of the church's staff working with the consultant. The consultant's role is to assist the church in developing concepts for implementing, but when the consultant has done their job, it is left in the hands of the local leadership of the church or denomination to actually implement and continuously maintain and evaluate the effectiveness of the model.

The best way for the church that desires to implement the DOT Model to understand the city is not only to read about it but to tour the city, perhaps many times. I would recommend that even if you lived in this city all your life, you should tour it because now you are looking for fresh winds of the Spirit that speak to you about an implementation strategy. This might involve undertaking a few paid sightseeing tours, having a native of the city take one to areas that the tour companies do not frequent and riding the public transportation system. In riding the public transportation system, one observes firsthand what communities are being served, who rides it, and what the surrounding businesses, industries, parks, and entertainment centers are nearby.

In Washington, DC, I rode all 106.3 miles of the Metrorail system on the five different rail lines. Every inch of the sixty-four miles of the Capital Beltway were driven by me, and the airport terminals were visited. During these riding and walking excursions, continuous prayer was offered to ask God for direction and insight. I, along with others, conducted a prayer walk around the US Capitol, White House, and Supreme Court, which represents the legislative, executive, and judicial branches of our government in the United States. Today, we have small groups meeting one block from both the US Capitol and White House and one two blocks from the Supreme Court. In doing all of this, God opened my eyes to observe the details to exegete the city as they pertain to the DOT Model, but that was not enough.

The prospective implementer of the DOT Model must not only exegete the city and the transportation system, but must "eisegete" it as well. Theologically, eisegesis means "to read into" the biblical text, something that was not present in the text to give it a different meaning than was originally communicated. In almost every instance, theological eisegesis is looked upon in a negative way.

To "see the unseen" using the DOT Model, the ministry environment must be eisegeted or read into. The pastor, church, or denomination must not only see how the transportation system now exists but must envision it as an integral vehicle for decentralizing the church into small groups that are relational, evangelical, pastoral for community, and replicable (multiplication) in the middle of the infrastructural flaws. The eisegesis should not be attempted by one's own thought process or rationalization, but the eisegetical creativity must come from God.

When I rode the various forms of transportation in the Washington metro region, I "watched as well as prayed" so that the ministry setting could be eisegeted with heavenly intervention. Each mile of track and road were prayerful, and God began to open up creative thoughts of how to implement the DOT Model. When eisegetical intervention comes from God, He reimages the city and the possibilities for ministry.

Finally, those that design and adapt the DOT Model for their city should document their findings and experiences. This might be accomplished by journaling, recording, writing, and engaging cartographers to develop maps illustrating the DOT Model strategy for your ministry setting. Remember, the DOT Model is unique to each context. This being said, it is impossible to be certain about the time it would take to design and implement it for each city because of unknown variables (for example, the size of the city, number of modes of transportation, information readily available, population density). It will most likely take longer to develop a DOT Model design for New York City, London, or Tokyo than it might for Seattle, Bedford, England, or Yokota, Japan.

What is certain is that I want you, your church, and your denomination, to succeed wherever you are in the world in designing and implementing the DOT Model. Not only do I want you to succeed, but most importantly, God wants you to, as it is His church and not ours. We partner with God in what He is doing through His church on the earth.

There also should be a desire for the church that implements a transportation-based small group model to have a missional training track for those going into the harvest to start new churches. Every congregation experiences member turnover, and most are both recipients of turnover and the source from which the turnover originates. Some church members have a desire to realign their membership with another church in the city; for others, it may be because of relocation for a job or family situation, such as a marriage.

Seldom do churches like to see people leave the fold, but it is a reality of life. For those who happen to leave you, for whatever reason, give them your blessings and continue to lift them up in prayer as they pursue their new adventure in life. For those that desire to begin new churches, the leadership of your congregation or denomination might want to place a high priority on missionary training. If you do, this will ensure that new pastors are equipped to implement both the small group and DOT models.

I recognize, and so do the leaders of churches and denominations, that God still "calls out" new churches from within the existing assembly for His purpose and glory. For those that indicate they feel a desire to start new churches, we should want to help them be successful in their endeavor. Pastors, ministers, and existing churches have a biblical responsibility to equip and empower new pastors who will lead new churches and then pass on that empowerment and knowledge to others in their assemblies that find themselves called by God to start churches. This theology is embedded in the writing of the Apostle Paul to his protégé, Timothy, when he said, "And what you have heard from me through many witnesses entrust to faithful people who will be able to teach others as well" (2 Tim. 2:2).

There is an entire teaching philosophy on who should start a church and various assessments that usually take place, which is beyond the scope of this book. However, it is suggested that part of the equipping process for those leaving your congregations to begin churches in other cities, domestically or internationally, include at least the awareness of how a modified version of the DOT Small Group (Cell) Model may be beneficial to them in the harvest of souls and strengthening of relationships. After the initial implementation of the transportation small-group model for your church, or those that started other churches for your church or denomination, the DOT Model must be evaluated.

THE NEED FOR EVALUATION

Before evaluation can take place, there must be some goals to evaluate. Bob Logan writes that these goals should be SMART goals, which are *specific, measurable, achievable, related* to the vision, and within a *time frame*.[161] Teachers evaluate students by giving content tests and annual standardized achievement tests, and workers are evaluated in an annual review; however, many churches are evaluated, if at all, by counting how many people are coming to church on any given Sunday. If the church is growing numerically, then it is assumed to be healthy. However, this may not be the case.

What are the overall goals for your church or denomination, both short-term and long-term? Where would you like to be one year from now, three years from now, and five years into the future? How many small groups would you like to see in your church? What kind of small groups? How often will they multiply into new small groups? How will you measure the vitality of community in the small groups? How will you develop leaders for the groups? Who will coach the various small group leaders? How might the transportation-based small group system fit into your paradigm? Where will these transportation-based small groups be located? When will the larger celebration worship be held and how often? Who will shoulder the responsibility for achieving these goals? What methodology will you embrace to go about achieving these goals?

These are possible questions that you might want to keep in the forefront as you design the transportation-based small group network for your church or denomination and set goals. You most likely have thought of others to add to the list. Each of these questions is critical to reflect on and answer so that you can appropriately state your goals. One question remains to be asked: How will you know when you have, or have not, achieved each of the stated goals? This is where the process of evaluation will be helpful. Stated goals are good, but if they are not evaluated, goals are almost meaningless. In other words, stated goals must be evaluated.

Any evaluation should have at least two aspects: a benchmarking to see where the system is currently and other appraisals to measure change from the initial benchmarking and between evaluations. Ralph W. Tyler provides some insight to this in his book, *Basic Principles of Curriculum and Instruction*. While this is relevant to the academic environment, the concepts are applicable for businesses, governments, and churches.

> The concept of evaluation has two important aspects. In the first place, it implies that evaluation must appraise the behavior of students since it is change in these behaviors which is sought in education. In the second place, it implies that evaluation must involve more than a single appraisal at any one time since to see whether change has taken place, it is necessary to make an appraisal at an early point and other appraisals at later points to identify changes that may be occurring. Without knowing where the students were at the beginning, it is not possible to tell how far changes have taken place.... Hence, it is clear that an educational evaluation involves at least two appraisals

—one taking place in the early part of the educational program and the other at some later point so that change may be measured.[162]

If you are an existing assembly or denomination that has small groups within the confines of the church building and desire to transition them in the marketplace using the DOT Model, it would be advisable for you to obtain a snapshot assessment of the current system before you transition, in order to compare the two down the road. If your church does not currently have small groups and you are implementing them, then evaluation of the current structure is still recommended to compare later with the new small group structure to ascertain their effectiveness and the satisfaction of the church members. If you are starting a new church then the benchmarking process is easily determinable.

With stated goals evaluated, a church can easily measure their progress at given intervals to understand where they are and what needs to change. The frequency of evaluations is important in order to see if change has taken place from the benchmarking point or the last evaluation. I recommend that each church or denomination assess their progress in relation to stated goals, operation, and church health with a formal evaluation at least once a year. The need for and frequency of evaluations have been stated, but next what evaluation methods will your church adopt?

EVALUATION METHODS

The methods of evaluation should be formulated to correlate with the objectives that the church is attempting to assess and to create the opportunities for those goals to be achieved by the membership. Once the objective and opportunities exist, then the evaluation methods can be determined. Some of the instruments that can be used for evaluation purposes are questionnaires, interviews, and sampling. The design of the evaluation tools is significant and, to be useful, they must be objective, reliable, and valid. Tyler defines objectivity as:

> To what degree two different persons, presumably competent, would be able to reach similar scores or summaries when they had an opportunity to score or summarize the same records of behavior. If the scores or summaries vary markedly, depending upon who does the scoring or summarizing, it is clearly a subjective kind of appraisal and requires improvement in its objectivity in order to be a more satisfactory means of appraising a human behavior.[163]

The reliability of the evaluation instrument is determined by the sample size of the population evaluated, where a larger sample size may be needed to obtain reliability if the results of a smaller sample size are widely dispersed. The validity of the evaluation tool is the most important of the three criteria and is directly related to the method itself and whether or not it substantiates the desired outcome, given the other two factors of objectivity and reliability. There are two ways of assuring validity of the evaluation instrument, which Tyler delineates.

> Validity can be assured in one of two ways. One way is getting directly a sample of the kind of behavior to be measured.... This is known as "face validity"—the evaluation instrument is valid on the face of it because it directly samples the kind of behavior which it is desired to appraise. The other way of assuring validity is through correlating a particular evaluation device with the result obtained by a directly valid measure.[164]

One of the best instruments for measurement of church health is the Natural Church Development (NCD) Survey. The Natural Church Development survey, developed by Christian Schwarz (which was discussed in a previous chapter, with statistics provided), is the most comprehensive assessment of church health in the world. To date, over forty thousand churches on six continents have taken three or more NCD profiles, and the results for these churches are that they have increased the quality of church life (in all eight categories) by six points and experienced a 51 percent increase in church growth. The percentage of transfer growth decreased, the percentage of conversion growth increased, and the workload of the participating members, especially the leaders, has decreased significantly.[165] While the NCD is a tool that is recommended annually for measuring church health (including holistic small groups, which is the most important to your church), it does not measure the performance of the DOT Model independently, or jointly with the small group model.

I desired a preliminary assessment of how the small groups are working in integration with the DOT Model in its infancy. In October 2010, I composed a twenty-question survey entitled, "Small Group/Transportation Evaluation," and is presented in Appendix D. The first ten of these questions are related to the small group, and the second ten are related to the DOT Model and its integration with the small groups.

The survey sampled the seventeen people who were regularly attending one of our small groups. These samples consisted of two men and fifteen women who were in their mid-twenties to mid-fifties. Ethnically, the sample population is multicultural:

five are Caucasian; six are African American; two are Asian (Japanese and Philippino); two are Hispanic (Colombian and Salvadorian); and two are multi-racial (African American-Caucasian and Mexican-Jamaican). Of the seventeen sampled, sixteen people returned their surveys for a total response of 94.1 percent. The survey exhibits outstanding results. Out of those surveyed, 75.0 percent stated they were practicing Christians, 6.3 percent were practicing members of another faith tradition (Jewish), and 18.7 percent said they were believers in their faith tradition, but were not practicing.

Highlights of the responses for the questions pertaining to small groups yielded the following. When asked whether the small group meetings that met outside the church building made it easier for them to make the decision whether or not to attend the small group, 75.0 percent replied that it had no effect, while 25.0 percent said it made it easier. Having various options of where to attend the small group (because of working in one area of the region and living in another) was important to 75.0 percent, while 12.5 percent of the sample said it had no importance, and the remaining 12.5 percent said it did not matter. For the question that pertained to limiting the size of the group to ten people to make it helpful for group relationships and participation, 88.0 percent replied affirmatively, 6.0 percent said no, and 6.0 percent were unsure.

Those who felt empowered to have a voice and participate freely in the small group were represented by 93.8 percent of the sample, while 6.2 percent said it had no effect. Of those surveyed, 88.0 percent reported that human fellowship and interaction with other small group members was important, and 12.0 percent thought it was somewhat important. When asked to rate the curriculum in clarity and application for their daily life, 88.0 percent responded that the curriculum was excellent, and 12.0 percent thought it was fair. The question that pertained to having each of the smaller groups meet jointly (celebration) was responded to favorably by 75.0 percent of responders and it did not matter for 13.0 percent of the group. Another 6.0 percent were unsure, and the question was not answered by 6.0 percent of the sample size.

The survey questions related to transportation concentrate on the effectiveness of the DOT Model. When asked whether or not the small group was accessible to Metrorail or Interstate highways, 100 percent of the sample said yes, and 68.8 percent said that this was a significant factor in choosing whether or not to attend the group. The different modes of their commute were the following: 31.3 percent of the total traveled using a combination of automobile and Metrorail, with most parking in the Metro Station parking garages; 56.3 percent exclusively traveled by automobile; 6.2 percent by Metrorail only; and 6.2 percent journeyed in by bicycle. For those using Metrorail on all or a portion of their commute, their reasons to do so were cited as less stressful than driving, parking concerns, cost, time efficiency, accessibility to starting place of commute, and proximity to the small group location.

Those that began their commute to the small group exclusively from home represented 56.3 percent, 37.5 percent commuted exclusively from work, and 6.2 percent responded that the starting place of their commute was split between home and work. A total of 50.0 percent of the sample located the small group site five or more miles from where they began their commute, 43.8 percent replied that it was one to three miles, and 6.2 percent said it was less than one mile. The total one-way commute time to the small group is five to fifteen minutes for 25.0 percent, fifteen to thirty minutes for 25.0 percent, and thirty to sixty minutes for 50.0 percent of the sample. Of those sampled, 56.3 percent believed that they saved time in their overall commute and in their day by attending the small group and avoiding traffic congestion at peak hours, while 6.2 percent reported that they did not save any time, 12.5 percent were unsure, and 25.0 percent failed to answer the question.

Statistics received from this and any other evaluations must be analyzed, for, without analysis, the numbers are somewhat meaningless. It is similar to accountants that analyze financial statements. They look for results, either positive or negative, after which they attempt to rationally formulate explanations for these results, taking into account other information that may corroborate their findings.

The analysis of the results of this evaluation of our transportation-based small groups in Washington indicates to me that small groups are important to people, and the resulting empowerment they receive and the relationships derived from them are fostered when groups are not too large. Based on the evidence, there seems to be a longing for a larger fellowship experience of the small groups in the celebration experience. Also of importance is having the option to attend different venues because of residing in one area and working in another. This is possible when the venues all offer the same material.

What is significant for the DOT Model is that it is a viable model in that 100 percent of the responding sample conveyed that they believed that small group locations were accessible to the Metrorail, Interstates, or major highways, with the majority stating that this was a significant factor in choosing to attend the small group. This evaluation of the small group and transportation network (DOT Model) in Washington, DC, served as a benchmark for measuring progress in future evaluations. The same will be true for your church when you evaluate your transportation-based small group network. Further evaluations performed on a consistent basis will only assist to strengthen what you already have in place.

CONTINUOUS IMPROVEMENT PROCESS

One of the key takeaways from the evaluation process is to learn what is working and what is not working for your church or denomination in your ministry setting. For those items that need tweaking or a complete overhaul, a process must be in place to guide these changes. An untruth exists that, if things are working well, the process should not change. There must be continuous improvement for processes that are working well, and there must be discernment for future direction in order to correctly implement changes in the present. Changes are welcomed by some, but most are hesitant or resist change; therefore, change management must be well thought out, methodical, and communicated effectively.

SUMMARY

This book presented a strategy for considering a transportation-based regional network of small groups for your church or denomination in your geographic region. The overall purpose of this strategy is to facilitate community for your members amidst impediments of urbanization and traffic congestion by identifying prime locations for the formation of these groups along the transportation infrastructure. This not only fosters community but positions the small groups to be missional in the marketplace outside of the church building. This strategy is the DOT Small Group (Cell) Model^{SM}, which considers mobility, accessibility, proximity, and time efficiency.

In essence the DOT Model is a transportation model that functions as a delivery system for the small group model that your church has chosen. While both are stand-alone models, the power can be seen by the integration of both. The small group structure's goal is to maximize relationships, whereas the transportation strategy purpose is to expedite the opportunity for community to happen in the first place.

I illustrated the application of the DOT Model strategy by using Washington, DC, for demonstrating the concepts in this book. The Washington, DC, metropolitan area serves as a good representation for the model, as it is the home of 5.5 million people and is the most traffic-congested city in the United States. While there are too many variables for this to be a how-to book for your church and region, it does provide shades of insight for you to consider the DOT Model for your ministry's setting.

Might the DOT Model be adaptable to other cities in the United States, such as New York, Los Angeles, Chicago, Dallas-Fort Worth, Philadelphia, Houston, Miami-Fort Lauderdale, Atlanta, or Boston? What about its use for churches in Tokyo, Seoul, Mexico City, Sao Paulo, Buenos Aires, Lagos, Mumbai, Manila, Shanghai, Cape Town, London, Paris, Sydney, or Melbourne? What about other urban or rural areas in the world? More specifically, can this strategy work for your church? My advanced research of other global cities has informed me that the resources are there to implement this model in many locations around the world. However, how would you know whether it will work or not, if you do not at least prayerfully consider it?

I hope this book has stirred your creativity for reimaging your mission for your church and the people in your cities. I am praying for you as you discern God's will for your church and community. If you desire to contact me concerning the book, please feel free to do so. My contact information appears next. If my company, Donaldson and Associates, LLC, can be of any assistance on a consulting basis, the contact information appears in the final pages of this book. I trust that the possibilities may exist for you to create a transportation-based network of small groups for the glory and kingdom of God, because with God, all things are possible to those who believe.

CONTACT INFORMATION

Readers may contact the author via
e-mail at info@washingtonbcc.org or by phone at
703-644-8180, or find him online at
www.washingtonbcc.org and
http://smallgroupsbigcity.tateauthor.com

Donaldson and Associates, LLC
325 Garrisonville Road,
Ste. 106-211
Stafford, VA 22554-1544
(540) 361-2110
www.donaldsonandassoc.com
info@donaldsonandassoc.com

The Donaldson &
Associates team
concentrates in church
consulting bringing a
combined 50+ years in
ministry and 45+ years
in corporate accounting/
finance to assist your
ministry in getting to the
next level.

DONALDSON & ASSOCIATES, LLC

Church Consultants

+ **DOT Small Group (Cell) Model^{SM}**

 ➤ **Domestic & International**

+ **Small Group Development Strategy**

+ **U.S. Domestic Demographic Studies**

+ **Christian Coaching**

 ➤ **Leadership, Business & Personal**

+ **Strategic Planning**

+ **Church Planting Strategy**

+ **Church Health Assessments**

+ **Multicultural/Diversity Education Seminars**

+ **Premarital and Marriage Enrichment Assessments**

DOT Small Group (Cell) Model is a service mark of Donaldson and Associates, LLC. Registration has been applied for with the USPTO and is pending.

APPENDIX A

Washington Beltway Community Church, Inc.
DOT Small Group (Cell) Model sm
For the Washington, DC Metropolitan Region

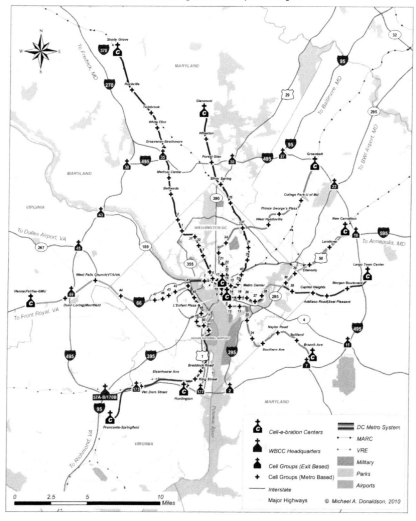

APPENDIX B

County	Location	Exit#	Symbol	Destinations
		Maryland		
Prince George's		2B		Interstate 295 North - Washington
	Oxon Hill	2A		Maryland Route 210 South - Indian Head
		3B		Maryland Route 210 (Indian Head Highway) - Indian Head, Forest Heights
	Marlow Heights	4A		Maryland Route 414 West (St. Barnabas Road) - Oxon Hill
		4B		Maryland Route 414 East (St. Barnabas Road) - Marlow Heights
	Andrews AFB	7A		Maryland Route 5 South (Branch Avenue) -

265

County	Location	Exit#	Symbol	Destinations
		7B		Waldorf Maryland Route 5 North (Branch Avenue) - Silver Hill
		9		Maryland Route 337 (Allentown Road) - Andrews AFB, Morningside
		11A		Maryland Route 4 - South/East (Pennsylvania Avenue) - Upper Marlboro
		11B		Maryland Route 4 - North/West (Pennsylvania Avenue) - Washington
	Ritchie	13		Ritchie-Marlboro Road - Upper Marlboro, Capitol Heights
	Largo	15A		Maryland Route 214 East (Central Avenue) - Largo
		15B		Maryland Route 214 West (Central Avenue) - Seat Pleasant
		16		Arena Drive

County	Location	Exit#	Symbol	Destinations
		17A		Maryland Route 202 East (Landover Road) - Upper Marlboro
		17B		Maryland Route 202 West (Landover Road) - Bladensburg
		19A		U.S. Route 50/I-595 East - Annapolis
		19B		U.S. Route 50 West - Washington
	New Carrollton	20A		Maryland Route 450 East (Annapolis Road) - Bladensburg
		20B		Maryland Route 450 West (Annapolis Road) - Lanham
	Greenbelt	22		Maryland Route 295 (Baltimore/Washington Parkway) North - Baltimore
		22		Maryland Route 295 (Baltimore/Washington Parkway) South - Washington, DC

County	Location	Exit#	Symbol	Destinations
		23		Maryland Route 201 (Kenilworth Avenue) - Bladensburg, Greenbelt
		24		Greenbelt Metro Station - Green Line
	Beltsville	25		U.S. Route 1 (Baltimore Avenue) - Laurel, Beltsville, College Park
		27		Interstate 95 North - Baltimore
Montgomery	Oakview	28A		Maryland Route 650 North (New Hampshire Avenue) - White Oak
		28B		Maryland Route 650 South (New Hampshire Avenue) - Takoma Park
	Silver Spring	29A		Maryland Route 193 West (University Boulevard) - Wheaton
		29B		Maryland Route 193 East (University Boulevard) - Langley Park
		30A		U.S. Route 29 North (Colesville Road) - Columbia

County	Location	Exit#	Symbol	Destinations
Montgomery (cont.'d)		30B		U.S. Route 29 South (Colesville Road) - Silver Spring
	Montgomery Hills	31		Maryland Route 97 - Georgia Avenue; Silver Spring, Wheaton
		33		Maryland Route 185 (Connecticut Avenue) - Chevy Chase, Kensington
	Bethesda	34		Maryland Route 355 (Wisconsin Avenue) - Bethesda, Rockville
		35		Interstate 270 North - Frederick
		36		Maryland Route 187 (Old Georgetown Road) - Bethesda, Rockville
		38		Interstate 270 Spur North - Rockville, Frederick
		39		Maryland Route 190 (River Road) - Washington, Potomac

County	Location	Exit#	Symbol	Destinations
	Cabin John	40		Cabin John Parkway - Glen Echo Carderock, Great Falls (Clara Barton Parkway North)
		41		Clara Barton Parkway - Carderock, Glen Echo
		41		

		Virginia		
Fairfax	Langley	43		George Washington Memorial Parkway - Washington State Route 193 (Old Georgetown Pike) - Langley, Great Falls
		44		
	McLean	45A		State Route 267 West - Dulles Airport
		45B		State Route 267 East to Interstate 66 East - Washington
		46A		State Route 123 South (Chain Bridge Road) - Tysons Corner, Vienna
		46B		State Route 123 North (Chain Bridge Road) - McLean

County	Location	Exit#	Symbol	Destinations
		47A		State Route 7 West (Leesburg Pike) - Tysons Corner
		47B		State Route 7 East (Leesburg Pike) - Falls Church
	Dunn Loring	49A-C		Interstate 66 West - Vienna, Front Royal
		49B		Interstate 66 East - Washington
	Fairfax	50A		U.S. Route 50 West (Arlington Boulevard) - Fairfax
		50B		U.S. Route 50 East, to U.S. Route 29 (Lee Highway) - Arlington
		51		State Route 650 (Gallows Road)
	Annandale	52A		State Route 236 West (Little River Turnpike) - Fairfax
		52B		State Route 236 East (Little River Turnpike) - Annandale
		54A		State Route 620 West (Braddock Road)
		54B		State Route 620 East

County	Location	Exit#	Symbol	Destinations
				(Braddock Road)
	Springfield	57A		Interstate 95 South - Richmond
		57B/170B		Interstate 395 North - Washington
				State Route 613 (State Route 401) (Van Dorn Street) -
		173		Franconia
		174		Eisenhower Avenue Connector - Alexandria
	Alexandria	176A		State Route 241 South (Telegraph Road)
		176B		State Route 241 North (Telegraph Road) - Alexandria
City of Alexandria		177A		U.S. Route 1 South - Alexandria, Fort Belvoir, Mount Vernon
		177B		U.S. Route 1 North - Old Town Alexandria

APPENDIX C

	WASHINGTON BELTWAY COMMUNITY CHURCH, INC.	
	DOT SMALL GROUP (CELL) MODEL℠	
	FOR THE WASHINGTON, DC METROPOLITAN REGION	
	METRORAIL - MAP KEY IN ASCENDING NUMERICAL STATION ORDER	

(A) All numerical idetified stations are in the District of Columbia and alpha identified stations are in suburban Maryland and Virginia

Map Label (A)	NAME	Route Served
1	Tenleytown-AU	RED LINE
2	Friendship Heights	RED LINE
3	Foggy Bottom|GWU	BLUE, ORANGE LINES
4	Farragut West	BLUE, ORANGE LINES
5	Farragut North	RED LINE
6	Dupont Circle	RED LINE
7	Woodley Park-Zoo|Adams Morgan	RED LINE
8	L'Enfant Plaza	BLUE, ORANGE LINES
9	Smithsonian	BLUE, ORANGE LINES
10	Federal Triangle	BLUE, ORANGE LINES
11	Archives-Navy Mem'l	GREEN, YELLOW LINES
12	Waterfront|SEU	GREEN LINE
13	Navy Yard	GREEN LINE
14	Federal Center SW	BLUE, ORANGE LINES
15	Judiciary Sq	RED LINE
16	Capitol South	BLUE, ORANGE LINES
17	McPherson Sq	BLUE, ORANGE LINES
18	Metro Center	RED LINE
19	Gallery Pl-Chinatown	RED LINE
20	Mt Vernon Sq - 7th St|Convention Center	GREEN LINE
21	U St/African-Amer Civil |War Memorial/Cardozo	GREEN LINE
22	Shaw-Howard Univ	GREEN LINE
23	Union Station	RED LINE
24	Congress Heights	GREEN LINE
25	Anacostia	GREEN LINE
26	Eastern Market	BLUE, ORANGE LINES
27	Potomac Ave	BLUE, ORANGE LINES
28	Stadium|Armory	BLUE LINE
29	Rhode Island Ave	RED LINE
30	Minnesota Ave	ORANGE LINE
31	Van Ness-UDC	RED LINE
32	Cleveland Park	RED LINE
33	Columbia Heights	GREEN LINE
34	Georgia Ave|Petworth	GREEN LINE
35	Takoma	RED LINE
36	Brookland-CUA	RED LINE
37	Fort Totten	GREEN LINE
38	Benning Road	BLUE LINE
39	Deanwood	ORANGE LINE
40	New York Ave	RED LINE
41	Rosslyn	BLUE, ORANGE LINES
42	Court House	ORANGE LINE
43	Clarendon	ORANGE LINE
44	East Falls Church	ORANGE LINE
45	Arlington|Cemetery	BLUE LINE

WASHINGTON BELTWAY COMMUNITY CHURCH, INC.
DOT SMALL GROUP (CELL) MODEL [SM]
FOR THE WASHINGTON, DC METROPOLITAN REGION
METRORAIL - MAP KEY IN ASCENDING NUMERICAL STATION ORDER

(A) All numerical idetified stations are in the District of Columbia and alpha identified stations are in suburban Maryland and Virginia

Map Label (A)	NAME	Route Served
46	Virginia|Square-GMU	ORANGE LINE
47	Ballston-MU	ORANGE LINE
48	Pentagon	YELLOW LINE
49	Pentagon City	BLUE, YELLOW LINES
50	Crystal City	BLUE, YELLOW LINES
51	Ronald Reagan Washington National Airport	BLUE, YELLOW LINES
Addison Road|Seat Pleasant	Addison Road|Seat Pleasant	BLUE LINE
Bethesda	Bethesda	RED LINE
Braddock Road	Braddock Road	BLUE, YELLOW LINES
Branch Ave	Branch Ave	GREEN LINE
Capitol Heights	Capitol Heights	BLUE LINE
Cheverly	Cheverly	ORANGE LINE
College Park-U of Md	College Park-U of Md	GREEN LINE
Dunn Loring|Merrifield	Dunn Loring|Merrifield	ORANGE LINE
Eisenhower Ave	Eisenhower Ave	YELLOW LINE
Forest Glen	Forest Glen	RED LINE
Franconia-Springfield	Franconia-Springfield	BLUE LINE
Glenmont	Glenmont	RED LINE
Greenbelt	Greenbelt	GREEN LINE
Grosvenor-Strathmore	Grosvenor-Strathmore	RED LINE
Huntington	Huntington	YELLOW LINE
King Street	King Street	BLUE, YELLOW LINES
Landover	Landover	ORANGE LINE
Largo Town Center	Largo Town Center	BLUE LINE
Medical Center	Medical Center	RED LINE
Morgan Boulevard	Morgan Boulevard	BLUE LINE
Naylor Road	Naylor Road	GREEN LINE
New Carrollton	New Carrollton	ORANGE LINE
Prince George's Plaza	Prince George's Plaza	GREEN LINE
Rockville	Rockville	RED LINE
Shady Grove	Shady Grove	RED LINE
Silver Spring	Silver Spring	RED LINE
Southern Ave	Southern Ave	GREEN LINE
Suitland	Suitland	GREEN LINE
Twinbrook	Twinbrook	RED LINE
Van Dorn Street	Van Dorn Street	BLUE LINE
Vienna|Fairfax-GMU	Vienna|Fairfax-GMU	ORANGE LINE
West Falls Church|VT/UVA	West Falls Church|VT/UVA	ORANGE LINE
West Hyattsville	West Hyattsville	GREEN LINE
Wheaton	Wheaton	RED LINE
White Flint	White Flint	RED LINE

APPENDIX D

WASHINGTON BELTWAY COMMUNITY CHURCH-SMALL GROUP/TRANSPORTATION EVALUATION

1. Which type of small group do you attend?

    ___ Topical Bible Series

    ___ Divorce or Grief Recovery

2. Where do you attend this small group?

    ___ Alexandria, VA

    ___ Arlington, VA

    ___ Washington, DC

    ___ Bethesda, MD

    ___ Springfield, VA

3. If applicable, does having various options of where to attend the small group important, because of working in one area of the region and living in another?

    ___ Yes ___ No ___ Does not matter

4. Do you believe having these small group meetings in facilities other than a church building made it easier for you to make the decision whether or not to attend the small group?
___Yes ___No ___ No Effect

5. Do you consider yourself to be one of the following?
___ Practicing Christian
___ Practicing member of another religious faith tradition
___ Believer in your faith tradition (Christian or other), but not practicing
___ Never been affiliated with a religious group
___ Agnostic (Is unsure if there is a God or not)
___ Atheist (Does not believe in God)

6. Do you think having a maximum of ten people in the group is helpful for group relationships and participation?
___Yes ___ No ___ Unsure

7. Do you feel empowered in having a voice and free to participate in the small group?
___Yes ___No ___ No Effect

8. How important to you is the human fellowship and interaction with other small group members?
   ___ Very Important
   ___ Somewhat Important
   ___ Not Important at all

9. How do you rate the curriculum in clarity and application for your daily life?
   Topical Bible Series:
   ___ Excellent
   ___ Fair
   ___ Poor

   DivorceCare and GriefShare:
   ___ Excellent
   ___ Fair
   ___ Poor

10. If attending a recovery group, do you believe it would be a good experience to bring our multiple small groups together in one place for a joint session (e.g., Surviving the Holidays Seminar)?
    ___Yes ___No ___Does not matter

11. Which type of transportation do you use to travel to the small group meetings?

___Metrorail

___ Metrobus or commuter-bus

___Combination of Rail/Bus

___Auto

___Combination of Auto/Rail

___Bicycle

___Walking

___ Other _____

12. Where is the starting point of your commute to the small group?

___Home

___ Work

___ School

___Other_____

13. How accessible is Metrorail or Bus Service to where you begin your commute?

If walking:

___ 1-2 blocks   ___3-5 blocks

___ 5-10 blocks   ___10 blocks or more

If driving:

___ less than 1mile   ___1-3 miles

___3-5 miles   ___ 5 miles or more

14. If Metrorail is your preferred mode of transportation to the small group, which factors influenced your decision
(Check all that apply)
___ less stressful than driving
___ parking concerns
___ cost
___ time efficiency
___ accessibility to starting place of commute
___ proximity to small group location
___ Other (explain) _____

15. In terms of proximity (closeness) what is the distance of the small group from where you start your commute?
___ 1-2 blocks   ___3-5 blocks
___ 5-10 blocks   ___10 blocks or more
___ less than 1mile   ___1-3 miles
___3-5miles   ___ 5 miles or more

16. How long in time is your commute to the small group location?
___ 5 Minutes or less   ___ 5-15 Minutes
__15-30 Minutes   ___ 30-60 Minutes
___Over 60 Minutes

17. Do you find the physical location of the small group to be accessible to Metrorail or major highways or Interstates?

    ___ Yes ___ No ___No Effect

    Was this a significant factor in choosing to attend the small group or not?

    ___ Yes ___No ___ No Effect

18. If you drive on any portion of your commute, where do you park?

    ___ Metrorail Station Parking Garage

    ___ Parking Garage in the small group location building or next-door

    ___ Street Parking near the small group location

19. How long in time is your commute home from the small group meeting?

    ___ 5 Minutes or less ___ 5-15 Minutes

    ___15-30 Minutes ___ 30-60 Minutes

    ___Over 60 Minutes

20. If you attend a small group closer to where you work or go to school, immediately after that function, do you believe you are saving time overall in the commute home because traffic congestion volume is lighter?

    ___Yes ___No ___Unsure

ABOUT THE AUTHOR

Dr. Michael A. Donaldson is the senior pastor of Washington Beltway Community Church, which is a multicultural church in the Washington, DC, metropolitan region. He emphasizes the power of pastoral care, evangelism, and relationships through small groups, with these groups coming together for corporate celebratory worship and fellowship. Mike's international research on small groups has convinced him that small, holistic groups empower everyone in the church to be blessed, but more importantly, to be a blessing to others as they participate in ministry.

Michael has participated in ministry for over thirty years. In the ministry, Michael has served in various capacities, including campus ministry, international youth ministry, Christian educator, hospital and airport chaplaincy, radio and television announcer, and pastor. He also has been fortunate to participate in the corporate finance/accounting sector for over thirty years, working in various industries for small, medium, and Fortune 500 companies, with most of these being in a managerial capacity.

Through this unique gift-mix Mike has been a blessing to the Church and the secular environment. He and his wife, Christy (who has a similar gift mix), have formed Donaldson and Associates, LLC, which specializes in church consulting. It is their desire to empower the Church in its mission to the world.

Mike attended and graduated from Fuller Theological Seminary, where he earned a Doctor of Ministry degree. He is also a graduate of Wake Forest University, where he earned a Master of Divinity degree, and is an alumnus of Marshall University, where he earned a Bachelor of Business Administration degree majoring in accounting. Mike is a volunteer chaplain at Ronald Reagan Washington National Airport in Washington, DC, and a member of several academic professional organizations. Michael; his wife, Christy; and their Yorkiepoo, Toby, live in suburban Virginia.

NOTES

1   This concept is analogous to that used by
medical researchers looking for a vaccination
to prevent or cure an infectious disease.
The pathology is studied for many years,
and then an antidote from a strain of
the virus itself is employed to immunize
the human body to that disease.

2   U.S. Census Bureau–2010 Census Information,
American Fact Finder. http://factfinder2.
census.gov/faces/nav/jsf/pages/index.
xhtml. (accessed February 18, 2012).

3   The National Congestion Tables of this report
ranked Washington, DC as number one in
the U.S. in yearly delay per auto commuter
with 74 hours. Texas Transportation Institute,
"2011 Urban Mobility Report," 20, http://tti.
tamu.edu/documents/mobility-report-2011-
wappx.pdf. (accessed February 18, 2012).

4   Wikipedia, "Washington Metro," http://
en.wikipedia.org/wiki/ Washington_
Metro (accessed August 15, 2011).

5   David Cho, *Successful Home Cell Groups* (Gainesville, FL: Bridge-Logos Publishers, 2001).

6   Joel Comiskey, *Home Cell Group Explosion: How Your Small Group Can Grow and Multiply* (Houston, Texas: Touch Publications, 2002), 17.

7   All Scripture quotations will be taken from the New Revised Standard Version of the Bible unless otherwise noted.

8   Randy Frazee, *The Connecting Church: Beyond Small Groups to Authentic Community* (Grand Rapids, MI: Zondervan Publishing House, 2001), 24.

9   Jack O. Balswick and Judith K. Balswick, *A Model for Marriage: Covenant, Grace, Empowerment and Intimacy* (Downers Grove, IL: IVP Academic, 2006), 15.

10 Jack O. Balswick and Judith K. Balswick, *The Family: A Christian Perspective on the Contemporary Home*, 3rd ed. (Grand Rapids, MI: Baker Academic, 2007), 311.

11 Washington DC: Population profile. http://www.city-data.com/us-cities/The-South/Washington-D-C-Population-Profile.html (accessed February 18, 2012).

12 U.S. Census Bureau – 2010 Census Information, American Fact Finder. http://factfinder2.census.gov/faces/nav/jsf/pages/index.xhtml. (accessed February 18, 2012).

13   Roger S. Greenway and Timothy M. Monsma,
      Cities: Missions' New Frontier, 2nd ed. (Grand
      Rapids, MI: Baker Books, 2000), 15-16.

14   I obtained this information in personal
      conversations with colleagues and friends.

15   U.S. Census Bureau–2010 Census Information,
      American Fact Finder.http://factfinder2.
      census.gov/faces/nav/jsf/pages/index.
      xhtml. (accessed February 18, 2012).

16   Ibid.

17   Wikipedia, "Baltimore-Washington
      Metropolitan Area," http://
      en.wikipedia.org/wiki/Baltimore
      %E2%80%93Washington_Metropolitan_
      Area.html (accessed August 15, 2011).

18   The Association of Religion Data Archives
      was founded in 1997. This is a highly
      professional organization, and the data
      included in the ARDA was submitted
      by the foremost religious scholars and
      research centers in the world.

19   The 188 groups of the ARDA survey refer
      to member organizations of a particular
      denomination. Some denominations
      stand alone as one organization (e.g.,
      Roman Catholic), while others have
      more than one (e.g. Baptist may be
      Southern, Primitive, National, etc.)

20   The Association of Religion Data
      Archives, "Metro Area Membership

Report–Washington-Baltimore, DC-MD-VA-WV CMSA," http://www.thearda.com/mapsReports/reports/metro/8872 _2000. asp.html (accessed August 15, 2011).

21   Wikipedia, "Baltimore-Washington Metropolitan Area."

22   Washington Beltway Community Church Mission Statement, adopted 2010.

23   Washington Beltway Community Church Vision Statement, adopted 2010.

24   Two major proponents are C. Peter Wagner and Donald McGavran. See the Lausanne Committee for World Evangelism, "Pasadena Consultation–Homogeneous Unit Principle," Lausanne Occasional Paper 1, <http://www.lausanne.org/all-documents/lop-1.html (accessed August 15, 2011).

25   Hozell C. Francis, *Church Planting in the African-American Context* (Grand Rapids, MI: Zondervan Publishing House, 1999), 102-103.

26   Jerry Appleby and Glen Van Dyne, *The Church Is in a Stew: Developing Multicongregational Churches* (Kansas City, MO: Beacon Hill Press of Kansas City, 1990), 22.

27   Some of the Cell Church Models are notably: Cho Model, 5x5, G-12, Department, Elim, D-4, G-12.3, G2 (squared), Free Market Small Group, J-12, Congregationally Focused, Blended Cell and Meta.

28   Robert E. Logan, *Be Fruitful and Multiply: Embracing God's Heart for Church Multiplication* (St. Charles, IL: Church Smart Resources, 2006), 19.

29   American Fact Finder. http://factfinder2.census.gov/faces/nav/jsf/pages/index.xhtml. (accessed February 18, 2012).

30   Ibid.

31   Ibid.

32   Ibid.

33   Ibid.

34   Ibid.

35   Ibid.

36   Ibid.

37   Ibid.

38   Ibid.

39   Ibid.

40   Ibid.

41   Ibid.

42   Robert Wuthnow, *After the Baby Boomers: How Twenty- and Thirty-Somethings Are Shaping the Future of American Religion* (Princeton, NJ: Princeton University Press, 2007), 212.

43   Harvie M. Conn, ed., *Planting and Growing Urban Churches: From Dream to Reality* (Grand Rapids, MI: Baker Books, 1997), 164-165.

44   The National Congestion Tables of this report
     ranked Washington, DC as number one in
     the U.S. in yearly delay per auto commuter
     with 74 hours. Texas Transportation Institute,
     "2011 Urban Mobility Report," 20, http://tti.
     tamu.edu/documents/mobility-report-2011-
     wappx.pdf. (accessed February 4, 2012).

45   U.S. Department of Transportation, Federal
     Highway Adminstration, Office of Operations,
     "Final Report, Traffic Congestion and
     Reliability: Trends and Advanced Strategies
     for Congestion Mitigation," chapter 2.2,
     http://ops.fhwa.dot.gov/congestion_report/
     chapter2.htm#2_2 (accessed August 15, 2011).

46   Ibid., chapter 3.

47   Wikipedia, "Interstate 495 (Capital Beltway),"
     http://en.wikipedia.org/wiki/Capital_
     Beltway; html (accessed August 15, 2011).

48   Wikipedia, "Springfield Interchange"
     http://en.wikipedia.org/wiki/Springfield_
     Interchange.html, (accessed August 15, 2011).

49   Howard A. Snyder, *The Problem
     of Wineskins: Church Structure in a
     Technological Age* (Downers Grove,
     IL: Inter-Varsity Press, 1975), 13.

50   Stanley J. Grenz, *Renewing the Center:
     Evangelical Theology in a Post-Theological
     Era*, 2nd ed. (Grand Rapids, MI: Baker
     Academic, 2006), 222-223.

51   Craig Van Gelder, ed., *The Missional Church in Context: Helping Congregations Develop Contextual Ministry* (Grand Rapids, MI: William B. Eerdmans Publishing Company, 2007), 107, referencing Avery Dulles, *Models of the Church*, expanded ed. (New York: Doubleday, 1987), 47. Dulles refers to C. H. Cooley, Introductory Sociology (New York: Scribners, 1933), 55.

52   Wikipedia, "Communitas," http://en.wikipedia.org/wiki/Communitas.html (accessed August 15, 2011).

53   Darrell L. Guder, ed., *Missional Church: A Vision for the Sending of the Church in North America* (Grand Rapids, MI: William B. Eerdmans Publishing Company, 1998), 23.

54   Gareth Weldon Icenogle, *Biblical Foundations for Small Group Ministry: An Integrational Approach* (Downers Grove, IL: InterVarsity Press, 1994), 27.

55   Bill Donahue and Russ Robinson, *Building a Church of Small Groups: A Place Where Nobody Stands Alone.* (Grand Rapids, MI: Zondervan, 2001), 23.

56   David Noel Freedman, ed., *The Anchor Bible Dictionary,* vol. 1. (New York, NY: Doubleday, 1992), 248.

57   Icenogle, *Biblical Foundations*, 21.

58   Donahue and Robinson, *Building a Church*, 41-42.

59   Icenogle, *Biblical Foundations*, 22.

60   Robert Banks, *Paul's Idea of
      Community,* rev. ed. (Peabody, MA:
      Hendrickson Publishers, 1998), 49.

61   Joseph H. Hellerman, *When the Church
      Was a Family: Recapturing Jesus' Vision for
      Authentic Christian Community.* (Nashville,
      TN: B&H Publishing Group, 2009), 31.

62   Ray Bakke, *A Theology as Big as
      the City* (Downers Grove, IL:
      InterVarsity Press, 1997), 61-63.

63   Ibid., 64.

64   Icenogle, *Biblical Foundations*, 52.

65   Joel Comiskey, *The Spirit-Filled Small
      Group: Leading Your Group to Experience
      the Spiritual Gifts* (Grand Rapids,
      MI: Chosen Books, 2005), 166.

66   Howard A. Snyder, *Liberating the Church:
      The Ecology of Church and Kingdom* (Eugene,
      OR: Wipf and Stock Publishers, 1996), 116.

67   Craig Van Gelder, *The Essence of the Church:
      A Community Created by the Spirit* (Grand
      Rapids, MI: Baker Books, 2000), 110.

68   William Edwy Vine, *An Expository
      Dictionary of New Testament Words*
      (Old Tappan, NJ: Fleming H. Revell
      Company, 1966), s.v. "church."

69   Howard A. Snyder, *The Community of the King* (Downers Grove, IL: InterVarsity Press, 1977), 169.

70   Bill Easum and Dave Travis, *Beyond the Box: Innovative Churches That Work* (Loveland, CO: Group Publishing, 2003), 70.

71   William A. Beckham, *The Second Reformation: Reshaping the Church for the 21st Century* (Houston, TX: Touch Publications, 1997), 25-26.

72   David J. Hesselgrave, *Planting Churches Cross-Culturally: North America and Beyond,* 2nd Ed. (Grand Rapids, MI: Baker Academic, 2006), 295.

73   M. Scott Boren and Don Tillman, *Making Cell Groups Work: Navigating the Transformation to a Cell-Based Church* (Houston, TX: Cell Group Resources, 2002), 75-76.

74   Robert Lewis and Rob Wilkins, *The Church of Irresistible Influence: Bridge-Building Stories to Help Reach Your Community* (Grand Rapids, MI: Zondervan, 2001), 190-191.

75   Wayne A. Meeks, *The First Urban Christians: The Social World of the Apostle Paul* (New Haven, CT: Yale University Press, 1983), 16-17.

76   Ibid., 16.

77   Ibid., 17.

78   Ibid., 18.

79   Ibid.

80   Greenway and Monsma, *Cities*, 55.

81   Harvie M. Conn and Manuel Ortiz,
     *Urban Ministry: The Kingdom, the City
     and the People of God* (Downers Grove,
     IL: InterVarsity Press, 2001), 244-245.

82   Reggie McNeal, *The Present Future:
     Six Tough Questions for the Church* (San
     Francisco, CA: Jossey-Bass, 2003), 8.

83   Reggie McNeal, *Practicing Greatness: 7
     Disciplines of Extraordinary Spiritual Leaders*
     (San Francisco, CA: Jossey-Bass, 2006), 75-76.

84   Gene A. Getz, *Sharpening the
     Focus of the Church* (Wheaton, IL:
     Victor Books, 1987), 222-223.

85   Ibid., 224-225.

86   Ibid., 225.

87   Michael C. Mack, *The Pocket Guide to
     Burnout-Free Small Group Leadership:
     How to Gather a Core Team and Lead
     from the Second Chair* (Houston, TX:
     Touch Publications, 2009), 25-26.

88   Icenogle, *Biblical Foundations*, 155, 157.

89   Robert E. Logan and Neil Cole, *Beyond
     Church Planting: Pathways for Emerging
     Churches: Knowing God – Loving Others
     – Growing the Kingdom* (St. Charles, IL:
     ChurchSmart Resources, 2005), 78.

90   Snyder, *The Problem of Wineskins*, 69.

91   Bart D. Ehrman, *The New Testament,*
      A Historical Introduction to the Early
      Christian Writings, 2nd ed. (New York, NY:
      Oxford University Press, 2000), 170.

92   Bruce J. Malina, "Dealing with Biblical
      (Mediterranean) Characters: A Guide
      for U.S. Consumers," *Biblical Theology*
      Bulletin (October 1989): 130.

93   Interestingly, according to Carolyn Osiek
      and David Balch, the rooms where slaves
      worked and slept in the house were called
      cells. Carolyn Osiek and David L. Balch,
      Families in the New Testament World:
      Households and House Churches (Louisville, KY:
      Westminster John Knox Press, 1997), 29.

94   Gerald F. Hawthorne, Ralph P. Martin, and
      Daniel G. Reid, eds., *Dictionary of Paul and*
      His Letters: A Compendium of Contemporary
      Biblical Scholarship (Downers Grove, IL:
      InterVarsity Press, 1993), 887-888.

95   Gerd Theissen, *The Social Setting*
      of Pauline Christianity (Edinburgh,
      Scotland: T&T Clark, Ltd., 1999), 83.

96   Stuart L. Love, *Families in the New*
      Testament World: Households and House
      Churches, vol. 61 of The Catholic Biblical
      Quarterly, Book Review (Malibu, CA:
      Pepperdine University, April 1999), 374.

97   Hawthorne, Martin and Reid,
      eds., *Dictionary of Paul*, 888.

98   Roger W. Gehring, *House Church and Mission: The Importance of Household Structures in Early Christianity* (Peabody, MA: Hendrickson Publishers, 2004), 187.

99   Neil Cole, "A Fresh Perspective of Paul's Missionary Strategies: The Mentoring for Multiplication Model" (Class handout for "Birthing and Multiplying Reproducing Churches," Fuller Theological Seminary, June 2007), 6.

100 Freedman, ed., *The Anchor Bible Dictionary*, vol. 3, 753.

101 Conn and Ortiz, *Urban Ministry*, 205-206.

102 Bakke, *A Theology*, 145-146.

103 Freedman, ed., *The Anchor Bible Dictionary*, vol. 6, 649.

104 Kirk C. Hadaway, Stuart A. Wright, and Francis M. Dubose, *Home Cell Groups and House Churches* (Nashville, TN: Broadman Press, 1987), 38.

105 Hawthorne, Martin, and Reid, eds., *Dictionary of Paul*, 125.

106 Robert Banks and Julia Banks, *The Church Comes Home* (Peabody, MA: Hendrickson Publishers, Inc., 1998), 29.

107 Ehrman, *The New Testament*, 37.

108 Grenz, *Renewing the Center*, 324-325.

109 Alvin Toffler, *Future Shock* (New York: Random House, 1970).

110   McNeal, *The Present Future*, xiii.

111   Grenz, *Renewing the Center*, 324-325.

112   Christian A. Schwarz, *Natural Church Development: A Guide to Eight Essential Qualities of Healthy Churches,* 6th ed. (St. Charles, IL: ChurchSmart Resources, 2003), 18.

113   Ibid., 33.

114   Dale Galloway and Kathi Mills, *The Small Group Book: The Practical Guide for Nurturing Christians and Building Churches* (Grand Rapids, MI: Fleming H. Revell, 1995), 14-15.

115   Richard Peace, "The Genius of a Small Group, Part I: The Design of Small Groups" from "Spiritual Formation and Discipleship in a Postmodern World" (Course material, Fuller Theological Seminary, 2008), 18.

116   Joel Comiskey, *Cell Church Solutions: Transforming the Church in North America* (Moreno Valley, CA: CCS Publishing, 2005), 20.

117   Cesar Castellanos, *Successful Leadership through the Government of 12* (Sunny Isles Beach, FL: G12 Publishers, 2002), 123.

118   Statistics provided by Church Initiative, Wake Forest, NC, licensor of DivorceCare, DivorceCare For Kids (DC4K) and GriefShare.

119 Wolfgang Simson, *Houses That Changed the World: The Return of the House Churches* (Waynesboro, GA: OM Publishing, 1988), 140.

120 Frazee, *The Connecting Church*, 89.

121 Malcolm Gladwell, *The Tipping Point: How Little Things Can Make a Big Difference* (New York: Bay Back Books, 2002), 179.

122 Ibid.

123 Ibid., 180-181.

124 Howard A. Snyder and Daniel V. Runyon, *Decoding the Church: Mapping the DNA of Christ's Body*. (Grand Rapids, MI: Baker Books, 2002), 65.

125 Washington Metropolitan Area Transit Authority, Media Relations Office, "Metro Media Guide 2010," http://www.wmata.com/about_metro/docs/2010_media_guide.pdf, pgs 17, 28 (accessed March 12, 2012).

126 Ibid., 18.

127 Ibid., 14.

128 Ibid., 18.

129 Ibid., 19.

130 Ibid.

131 Wikipedia, "Interstate 495 (Capital Beltway)," http://en.wikipedia.org/wiki/Capital_Beltway; html (accessed August 15, 2011).

132 Wikipedia, "Springfield Interchange" http://en.wikipedia.org/wiki/Springfield_ Interchange.html (accessed August 15, 2011).

133 Maryland State Highway Administration, Highway Information Services Division, "2010 Traffic Volume Maps by County," http:// sha.md.gov/Traffic_Volume_Maps/Traffic_ Volume_Maps.pdf (accessed August 15, 2011).

134 Commonwealth of Virginia, Department of Transportation, "Average Daily Traffic Volumes with Vehicle Classification Data on Interstates, Arterial and Primary Roads," http://virginiadot.org/info/resources/2010/ AADT_PrimaryInterstate_2010. pdf (accessed February 16, 2012).

135 Washington MATA, "Metro Media Guide 2010." 19.

136 Ibid., 15.

137 Ibid., 16, 20.

138 The Phrase Finder, http://www. phrases.org.uk/meanings/255800. html (accessed August 15, 2011).

139 http://www.wmata.com/pdfs/planning/ Historical%20Rail%20Ridership%20By%20 Station.pdf (accessed August 15, 2011).

140 http://en.wikipedia.org/wiki/ Union_Station_(Washington,_D.C.) (accessed August 15, 2011).

141 Ibid.

142   Washington MATA, "Metro
      Media Guide 2010," 19.

143   Ibid.

144   Ibid.

145   Ibid.

146   http://www.wmata.com/pdfs/planning/
      Historical%20Rail%20Ridership%20By%20
      Station.pdf (accessed August 15, 2011).

147   Ibid.

148   Ibid.

149   Washington MATA, "Metro
      Media Guide 2010" 19.

150   http://www.wmata.com/pdfs/planning/
      Historical%20Rail%20Ridership%20By%20
      Station.pdf (accessed August 15, 2011).

151   Washington MATA, "Metro
      Media Guide 2010" 19.

152   http://www.wmata.com/pdfs/planning/
      Historical%20Rail%20Ridership%20By%20
      Station.pdf (accessed August 15, 2011).

153   Wikipedia, "Washington Metro," http://
      en.wikipedia.org/wiki/Washington_Metro.
      html (accessed August 15, 2011).

154   Ibid.

155   Ibid.

156   Ibid.

157   Ibid.

158   Ibid.

159   Ray Bakke and Jon Sharpe, *Street Signs: A New Direction in Urban Ministry* (Birmingham, AL: New Hope Publishers, 2006), 96-97.

160   Ibid., 99.

161   Logan and Cole, *Beyond Church Planting*, 107.

162   Ralph W. Tyler, *Basic Principles of Curriculum and Instruction* (Chicago, IL: The University of Chicago Press, 1969), 106.

163   Ibid., 117-118.

164   Ibid., 119.

165   Natural Church Development, "Frequently Asked Questions: Results What Have Been the Benefits of NCD So Far?" http://www.ncd-international.org/public/FAQ-Results.html (accessed August 15, 2011).

listen|imagine|view|experience

AUDIO BOOK DOWNLOAD INCLUDED WITH THIS BOOK!

In your hands you hold a complete digital entertainment package. In addition to the paper version, you receive a free download of the audio version of this book. Simply use the code listed below when visiting our website. Once downloaded to your computer, you can listen to the book through your computer's speakers, burn it to an audio CD or save the file to your portable music device (such as Apple's popular iPod) and listen on the go!

How to get your free audio book digital download:

1. Visit www.tatepublishing.com and click on the e|LIVE logo on the home page.
2. Enter the following coupon code:
   12ca-c46f-5f17-9fc3-7636-c571-fdbe-4d1f
3. Download the audio book from your e|LIVE digital locker and begin enjoying your new digital entertainment package today!